150 best
grilled cheese
sandwiches

150 best grilled cheese sandwiches

Alison Lewis

Robert
ROSE

For complete cataloguing information, see page 213

Disclaimer

The recipes in this book have been carefully tested by our kitchen and our tasters. To the
best of our knowledge, they are safe and nutritious for ordinary use and users. For those
people with food or other allergies, or who have special food requirements or health issues,
please read the suggested contents of each recipe carefully and determine whether or not
they may create a problem for you. All recipes are used at the risk of the consumer.

We cannot be responsible for any hazards, loss or damage that may occur as a result of
any recipe use.

For those with special needs, allergies, requirements or health problems, in the event of
any doubt, please contact your medical adviser prior to the use of any recipe.

Design and Production: Kevin Cockburn/PageWave Graphics Inc.
Editor: Carol Sherman
Consulting Editor: Jennifer MacKenzie
Copy Editor: Karen Campbell-Sheviak
Photography: Colin Erricson
Associate Photographer: Matt Johannsson
Food Styling: Kathryn Robertson
Prop Styling: Charlene Erricson

Cover image: Classic Grilled Two Cheese (page 80)

Additional photography: © shutterstock.com/Nayashkova Olga (Assorted Cheese #1),
© iStockphoto.com/John Peacock (Bread #1), © iStockphoto.com/fatihhoca (Bread #2),
© shutterstock.com/NADKI (Assorted Cheese #2), © iStockphoto.com/Ivan Mateev (Assorted
Cheese #3), © iStockphoto.com/atılay ünal (Bread #3), © shutterstock.com/Wiktory (Basil
Pesto), © shutterstock.com/Wiktory (Hummus)

We acknowledge the financial support of the Government of Canada through the Book
Publishing Industry Development Program (BPIDP) for our publishing activities.

Published by Robert Rose Inc.
120 Eglinton Avenue East, Suite 800, Toronto, Ontario, Canada M4P 1E2
Tel: (416) 322-6552 Fax: (416) 322-6936
www.robertrose.ca

Printed and bound in Canada

1 2 3 4 5 6 7 8 9 FP 20 19 18 17 16 15 14 13 12

Dedicated to my parents,
Alvin and Audrey Rich

Contents

Acknowledgments

I want to start by thanking my agent, Lisa Ekus, and all of her incredible staff at the Lisa Ekus Group, as well as Bob Dees, publisher of Robert Rose books, for this second cookbook opportunity. I know I am always sending you both countless ideas, and I am honored to have two cookbooks released in two years. I also appreciate my editor, Carol Sherman, for her diligent, incredible, and endless hours of help and attention to detail. I am thrilled to have you as an editor twice. Thanks to Jennifer Mackenzie and Karen Campbell-Sheviak for proofing my recipes and offering helpful suggestions. Thank you to everyone at PageWave Graphics, including designer Kevin Cockburn, for making another beautiful book, and to photographer Colin Erricson for the fabulous grilled cheese photographs.

Special thanks to friends and assistants who helped with recipe ideas, testing and support, including Nancy Bynon, Alatia Butler, Caroline Downing, Jessica Segarra, Kelley Epstein, Kiel Gross and Lisa Goldstein. I also thank all of my blog subscribers, Facebook friends, Twitter followers and blogger friends for their continued support of all of my work.

A huge thank you always goes out to my sisters, Julie and Natalie, and my brother, Craig, for their faithful support in everything I do and excitement over this project. I can't thank my parents, Alvin and Audrey Rich, enough (to whom this book is dedicated). Both of them have been very ill, and I pray for their peace and health.

Most of all, I want to thank Jon Lewis for his endless support with everything I do in life. He continues to be my constant cheerleader, a great father and my best friend. I also don't know how to thank my three children, Alec, Leigh and Zachary, who are growing up so fast. When I told them I was doing a grilled cheese book, they had the biggest smile. I love all of you so much, and words can't express my love and gratitude for everyone listed above.

Introduction

Having the opportunity to have two published cookbooks in a two-year span is an incredible feeling and truly, a dream. I was more than ecstatic when my agent, Lisa Ekus, and publisher, Bob Dees, said they wanted me to do a grilled cheese cookbook to be released in 2012. When I was thinking about selling points for this cookbook, I was thrilled to see grilled cheese on so many 2012 trend lists. There has been a huge resurgence of grilled cheese sandwiches on restaurant menus across the globe. Also, grilled cheese food trucks have popped up everywhere from Florida to Los Angeles.

Grilled cheese has been called the "new hamburger," and I can see why. My friend Kelley, a personal chef and food blogger in Utah, said recently, "Grilled cheese makes the world a better place." When she tweeted this quote, it sent a flurry of other tweets of agreement and those tweets added comments suggesting what to add to make the grilled cheese (and the world) even better (such as bacon). She was truly correct in that statement.

Grilled cheese sandwiches are not only one of North America's top comfort foods, but they are also nostalgia based. Most people immediately think back to their childhoods and how their moms used to make them. Eating grilled cheese sandwiches really gets people in touch with their five senses as well as their memory. What other food can make you say that? Research shows that two billion grilled cheese sandwiches are eaten in U.S. homes each year. Today, we have so many incredible options of artisan and healthy breads and cheeses to choose from. The possibilities are virtually endless... and delicious. Here are more than 150 recipes for grilled cheese sandwiches and condiments to get you started. From breakfast to dessert, there's something for everyone in this book.

Grilled Cheese Basics

History of the Grilled Cheese Sandwich

According to food historians, cooked cheese and bread is an ancient food popular around the world. Dating back to 1920, the modern version of the grilled cheese sandwich evolved when inexpensive sliced bread and American cheese became popular in the great depression, often called the "Cheese Dream" and served as an inexpensive company supper dish. Originally, it was made as an open-faced sandwich. Navy cooks were making grilled cheese sandwiches during World War II, but the top slice of bread wasn't commonly used until the early 1960s.

Choosing the Best Cheese

The main criteria for choosing your cheese is whether it's good melting cheese as well as combining the flavor of the cheese with your other ingredients. The more your cheese melts, the better it is. Choose the best, freshest cheese available for best results.

Easy melting cheeses can be found most anywhere and include American, Brie, Cheddar, Colby, fontina, Gouda, Gruyère, Havarti, Jarlsberg, Monterey Jack, mozzarella, Muenster, provolone and Swiss. Other cheeses that melt and pack great flavor include Asiago, blue cheese, goat cheese, Gorgonzola and Parmigiano-Reggiano.

Storing Cheese

To store cheese, place in the refrigerator. Plastic packaging is only good for a short term because it doesn't let the cheese breathe. If left too long, bacteria will build up on the cheese's surface. If cutting whole large cheese, cover only the cut area with plastic wrap. If storing firm, semifirm or semisoft cheeses, wrap tightly in a plastic bag or foil. Store in the refrigerator's cheese compartment for up to several weeks, or check the due date on the package. Soft cheeses should be tightly wrapped, but even then, they only last for several days. Semifirm cheeses, such as Cheddar, Swiss and Monterey Jack, are easier to grate when they are cold.

Breads

Great breads make great grilled cheese sandwiches. Try to match breads that pair well with your cheese in thickness and in flavor. Thick slices of bread require thick slices of cheese. Bread options are limitless. You can use freshly baked bread or any of your favorite store-bought or bakery breads.

Whole-grain breads are healthier and provide more fiber so they make you feel fuller longer. They work great in recipes such as my favorite Grilled Peach and Brie (page 47) or Grilled Pear and Swiss (page 24).

Sourdough and **Italian breads** are always fabulous choices, pairing well with many mild and strong-flavored cheeses, such as Turkey Antipasto Grilled Cheese (page 125) or Grilled Roast Beef and Sweet Pepper Relish (page 100).

Pita, tortillas and **flatbreads** make healthier, lighter choices (and the kids love them) in recipes, such as Grilled Mascarpone, Banana and Honey (page 205) or Broccoli Cheese Pitas (page 73).

Fruity breads, such as raisin bread, work well in many grilled cheese sandwiches, such as Muenster-Stuffed Raisin Bread (page 29).

Brioche and **challah breads** provide rich egg flavor and awesome texture. Choose these when making dessert or French toast-type grilled cheese recipes such as Grilled Chocolate and Goat Cheese (page 203).

Bagels, English muffins and **croissants** are not just for breakfast recipes. Using them is always a great, new twist and a way to use up leftover breads. My kids are wild about the Grilled Smoked Salmon Bagel (page 36) and Raspberry and Chocolate Grilled Cheese (page 210).

Focaccia, ciabatta and **French bread** take a typical grilled cheese to a new level, such as in the Seasonal Vegetable Panini (page 86), Muffuletta Grilled Cheese (page 150), and so many crostini recipes in the appetizer chapter.

Basic white bread is always a hit with kids and adults alike, making finger sandwiches and your typical grilled cheese, such as the Classic Grilled Two Cheese (page 80) and the Southwestern Grilled Cheese (page 84).

Round sandwich thins are made by many major brand companies and are packed in bags in the bread section. They are great for regular and mini grilled cheese sandwiches.

Gluten free bread: For those of you who eat a gluten-free diet, feel free to choose your favorite variety of gluten-free bread. The quality of gluten-free breads has changed for the better dramatically over the years, and a wealth of options are now available. The "multigrain" breads are usually richer and more satisfying. You can also find soft rolls, French-style baguettes and white breads, sprouted breads and more.

Storing Bread

For best results, store bread at room temperature in a cool, dry place. Store homemade breads by wrapping the bread very tightly in a couple of layers of plastic wrap, and store in a cool, dark place.

Sandwich Toppings

Choose great toppings for your sandwiches to add texture, flavor and crunch.

Vegetables

Vegetables, such as cucumbers, lettuces, sprouts, mushrooms, onions and tomatoes, add huge flavor, color, texture and depth to grilled cheese sandwiches. Use the freshest lettuce varieties you can find, and experiment with different types such as arugula, watercress and baby spinach. Roasting vegetables also gives them great flavor without adding a lot of fat. Choose wonderful selections such as Broccoli Cheese Pitas (page 73), Tabbouleh Quinoa Feta Melts (page 75) or Grilled Veggie and Goat Cheese Wraps (page 70).

Fruits

Fresh fruits make a terrific grilled cheese sandwich component. Try apples on the Grilled Brie, Apple and Thyme (page 45), raspberries in the Brie and Raspberry Panini with Hazelnut Spread (page 206), or strawberries in the Grilled Balsamic-Strawberry and Mascarpone Sandwich (page 207). Dried fruits also add texture to grilled cheese sandwiches and preserves add great flavor when fresh fruit isn't in season.

Condiments

Homemade spreads, sauces, salsas and chutneys add wonderful flavor and texture to sandwiches. From pestos, aïolis and flavored cream cheese, there's something for everyone. The condiment chapter starts on page 175, and some of my favorites are the Garlic-Herb Cream Cheese (page 197) served on the Grilled Smoked Salmon and Bagel (page 36) and the Peach-Ginger Chutney (page 176) served on Grilled Cheese and Peach-Ginger Chutney (page 62).

Grilled Cheese Tips

- Spread softened butter on the bread instead of adding it to the pan. This will keep the butter from burning.
- Use grated, shredded or thinly sliced cheese for quicker melting.
- Slice and grate the cheese when it's cold, but cheese melts better when it's brought to room temperature.
- The more cheese, the better the result.
- If the cheese hasn't melted by the time the bread is golden, turn off the heat, and let stand, covered, until the cheese melts.
- Use your favorite bread, and don't slice it too thick. I prefer $\frac{1}{2}$- to 1-inch (1 to 2.5 cm) thick slices.

Cooking Tips

- Using a good panini maker makes a difference. You can also cook grilled cheese sandwiches or paninis in a heavy skillet, and press down with a metal spatula on the top.
- A good metal spatula makes for easy turning and helps the bread stay intact. Having such a spatula also helps ensure that the ingredients don't fall out of the sandwich.
- It is helpful to have all of the ingredients assembled ahead of time.
- Go for slow, even cooking. Don't rush it and burn your bread.
- When using a panini grill, large skillet or grill, make sure it's hot enough before you use it.
- Try not to pack too many ingredients in a sandwich so they don't fall out, especially when you're using a roll or baguette.
- Let the cheese ooze. If some cheese comes out, that is OK. Enjoy.
- Don't forget to remove the rind of the cheese. Do this when the cheese is cold.
- Use your favorite combinations. Have fun, and be creative.

Low-Fat and Lightening-Up Tips

- Use lean cuts of beef, chicken, fish and white meat poultry.
- Use fillings that add little fat but lots of flavor, such as lettuce, spinach, arugula, tomato, cucumbers, etc.
- Use nonstick skillets or spray with cooking spray to cut down on the oil or butter needed in the pan.
- Use reduced-fat tortillas, breads, cheeses and lean deli meats.
- Substitute reduced-fat mayonnaise and cream cheese for the regular versions.
- Grainy mustards, chutney, low-fat and Greek yogurt make great toppings without adding a lot of fat.
- Use fresh herbs, sun-dried tomatoes, capers, vinegars and freshly ground pepper for adding robust flavors.
- My favorite sandwich toppers are arugula, sprouts, tomatoes, pears, radishes, cucumbers, apples, green onions, sunflower seeds, sweet peppers and turkey.

Sandwich Shortcuts

When creating recipes, I try to come up with the best possible results with time-savers. Here are some shortcut tips:

- Gather all of your ingredients before you begin.
- Make very organized grocery lists. I like to create my list by the way the store is laid out.
- Use a panini grill, grill, grill pan or large skillet.
- Grate the cheese onto waxed or parchment paper. This makes it easy to transport and cleanup is a snap.
- Grate the cheese ahead of time. The day before, grate and wrap in plastic wrap and store in the refrigerator. Bring it to room temperature before using.
- Use a nonstick skillet. It will cook hotter and faster.
- Use pre-cut carrots, sliced mushrooms and bagged, washed greens.
- Use chicken cutlets or thinly sliced pork because they cook quicker.
- Use rotisserie chicken to save time on cooking.
- Purchase fresh or frozen shrimp that has already been peeled and deveined.
- Purchase extra meats to freeze for later use.
- Get the kids involved because it provides help in the kitchen, and they get excited about what you're making.

Seasonal Options

- *Fall:* Choose autumn produce such as mushrooms, pears, herbs, apples and nuts.
- *Winter:* Choose greens, apples, pears, citrus fruits and pineapple.
- *Spring:* Try leafy greens, fresh herbs and berries.
- *Summer:* Enjoy tomatoes, corn, peaches, figs, nectarines, peaches, melons and herbs.

Cutting Sandwiches

Slice grilled cheeses normally in triangles, halves or quarters. For something new and different, try these other options:

- *Finger sandwiches:* Cut crust off bread and cut into 2-inch (5 cm) strips. Assemble in skillet or panini grill, and cook for a little less time.
- *Rounds:* Cut crusts off bread, and cut with a biscuit or cookie cutter into circles. Then, assemble your sandwiches. They will cook in less time.
- *Triangles:* Remove the crust from bread, and cut into diagonal halves before assembling and cooking.
- *Shapes:* Use your favorite cookie cutter to create new shapes before assembling and cooking.

Breakfast and Brunch

Grilled Goat Cheese and Figs

Serves 4

This is one of my favorites in the summertime when figs are in season. The combination of figs and goat cheese makes a delectable sandwich.

- **Panini grill or large skillet**
- **Preheat panini grill to medium, if using**

8	slices raisin bread (1/2-inch/1 cm thick slices)	8
2 tbsp	butter or margarine, softened	30 mL
1/4 cup	fig preserves or jam	60 mL
4 tsp	liquid honey	20 mL
4 oz	crumbled goat cheese	125 g

1. Brush one side of each bread slice with butter. Place on a work surface, buttered side down. Spread tops of 4 bread slices equally with fig preserves, honey and goat cheese. Cover with remaining bread slices, buttered side up, and press together gently.

2. Place sandwiches on preheated panini grill or in a large skillet over medium heat and cook, turning once if using a skillet, for 3 to 4 minutes or until golden brown and cheese is melted. Serve immediately.

Variation

If you can't find fig preserves, substitute peach, apricot or strawberry preserves or jam.

Grilled Apple and Cheddar Sandwich

Serves 4

This is a twist on an old-fashioned Cheddar pie recipe, and it makes a fabulous sweet and savory warm sandwich.

- **Panini grill or large skillet**
- **Preheat panini grill to medium, if using**

8	slices multigrain bread ($\frac{1}{2}$-inch/1 cm thick slices)	8
$\frac{1}{4}$ cup	butter or margarine, softened	60 mL
$\frac{1}{4}$ cup	liquid honey	60 mL
2	apples, thinly sliced	2
8	slices sharp (aged) Cheddar cheese	8

1. Brush one side of each bread slice with butter. Place on a work surface, buttered side down. Spread 4 bread slices equally with honey. Top equally with apple slices and cheese. Cover with remaining bread slices, buttered side up, and press together gently.

2. Place on panini grill or in a skillet over medium heat and cook, turning once if using skillet, for 3 to 4 minutes until cheese is melted. Serve immediately.

Grilled Apple and Blue Cheese Sandwich

This sandwich says fall with the mixture of apples, walnuts and blue cheese. If you can't find apple preserves, apricot is a nice substitute.

Tips

To toast walnuts: Toasting nuts intensifies their flavors. I like to toast mine in a skillet over medium heat, tossing gently, for 3 to 5 minutes or in a 350°F (180°C) oven for 5 to 10 minutes or until fragrant and golden brown.

If you like a less potent blue cheese flavor, reduce the blue cheese to 2 tbsp (30 mL).

- **Panini grill or large skillet**
- **Preheat panini grill to medium, if using**

4 oz	cream cheese, softened	125 g
3 tbsp	crumbled blue cheese	45 mL
2 tbsp	apple preserves or apple jelly	30 mL
4 tsp	liquid honey	20 mL
8	slices whole wheat bread or oat bread (1/2-inch/1 cm thick slices)	8
1/4 cup	butter or margarine, softened	60 mL
2	Gala apples, thinly sliced	2
1 cup	mesclun lettuce or mixed spring greens	250 mL
1/2 cup	chopped toasted walnuts (see Tips, left)	125 mL

1. In a small bowl, combine cream cheese and blue cheese. Set aside.

2. In a separate bowl, combine apple preserves and honey. Brush one side of each bread slice equally with butter. Place bread on work surface, buttered side down. Spread preserve mixture equally on half of bread slices and cream cheese mixture on the other halves. Top 4 slices with apples, lettuce and walnuts. Cover with remaining bread slices, buttered side up, and press gently.

3. Place sandwiches on preheated panini grill or in a large skillet over medium heat and cook, turning once if using a skillet, for 3 to 4 minutes or until golden brown and cheese is melted. Serve immediately.

Grilled Apricot Blues

Serves 4

Believe it or not, my kids love blue cheese and apricots. I created this sandwich for them one day, and it was gone within minutes.

Tip

If you have leftover blue cheese, use it in salads, on vegetables, on top of burgers or steak and in salad dressings.

- **Panini grill or large skillet**
- **Preheat panini grill to medium, if using**

8	slices sourdough bread (1/2-inch/1 cm thick slices)	8
2 tbsp	butter or margarine, softened	30 mL
1/4 cup	apricot preserves or jam	60 mL
1 cup	spinach leaves	250 mL
3/4 cup	dried apricots	175 mL
4 oz	crumbled blue cheese	125 g

1. Brush one side of each bread slice with butter. Place on a work surface, buttered side down. Spread 4 slices equally with apricot preserves. Top equally with spinach leaves, apricots and blue cheese. Cover with remaining bread slices, buttered side up, and press together gently.

2. Place sandwiches on preheated panini grill or in a large skillet over medium heat and cook, turning once if using a skillet, for 3 to 4 minutes or until golden brown and cheese is melted. Serve immediately.

Grilled Pear and Swiss Cheese

Serves 4

Celebrate fresh pears in fall with this super easy, warm and comforting sandwich.

Tip

Feel free to use any of your favorite pear varieties.

- **Panini grill or large skillet**
- **Preheat panini grill to medium, if using**

8	slices multigrain bread ($\frac{1}{2}$-inch/1 cm thick slices)	8
$\frac{1}{4}$ cup	butter or margarine, softened	60 mL
$\frac{1}{4}$ cup	honey mustard	60 mL
2	pears, thinly sliced (see Tip, left)	2
1 cup	arugula or spinach leaves	250 mL
4	slices Swiss cheese	4

1. Brush one side of each bread slice with butter. Place on a work surface, buttered side down. Spread 4 bread slices equally with honey mustard. Top 4 slices equally with pears, arugula and cheese. Cover with remaining bread slices, buttered side up, and press together gently.

2. Place sandwiches on preheated panini grill or in a large skillet over medium heat and cook, turning once if using a skillet, for 3 to 4 minutes or until golden brown and cheese is melted. Serve immediately.

Open-Faced Nectarine and Chèvre Sandwich

Serves 4

These sandwiches are perfect in the summertime as an appetizer, breakfast or dessert sandwich when nectarines are at their peak season.

Tips

Don't worry about removing the skin from the nectarines. It gives it more texture.

To toast pecans: Spread nuts in a single layer on a baking sheet. Bake in a preheated 350°F (180°C) oven, stirring occasionally, for 10 to 15 minutes.

If you're grilling during the summertime, grill the bread slices over medium heat, turning once, for 1 to 2 minutes or until grill marks appear.

• **Preheat broiler with rack 4 inches (10 cm) from heat**

4	slices multigrain bread (½-inch/1 cm thick slices), toasted	4
2 tbsp	olive oil	30 mL
4 oz	goat cheese, at room temperature	125 g
3	medium nectarines, thinly sliced (see Tips, left)	3
4 tsp	liquid honey	20 mL
¼ cup	chopped pecans, toasted (see Tips, left)	60 mL

1. Brush one side of each bread slice with olive oil. Spread each slice equally with goat cheese. Broil for 1 to 2 minutes or until lightly toasted.

2. Arrange nectarine slices on top of bread slices and drizzle with honey. Sprinkle with pecans and serve open-faced. Serve immediately.

Variations

Gluten-Free Summer Chèvre Sandwich: Substitute gluten-free bread for the multigrain bread.

Substitute 2 medium peaches or 4 small plums for the nectarines in this recipe.

Strawberry and Mascarpone Sandwich

Spring is the perfect time to make this breakfast sandwich. Top with fresh mint for added color.

What to do with Mascarpone

- Serve with cantaloupe
- Stir it into pasta
- Serve with poached pears or baked apples
- Mix with Gorgonzola and spread on crackers
- Stir into cheesecake mixtures
- Serve on top of toasted bread
- Eat with a spoon
- Use in parfaits
- Use a spread in panini sandwiches

- **Panini grill or large skillet**
- **Preheat panini grill to medium, if using**

8	slices Italian bread (1/2-inch/1 cm thick slices)	8
2 tbsp	butter, softened	30 mL
1/2 cup	mascarpone cheese	125 mL
2 tbsp	liquid honey	30 mL
2 1/2 cups	thinly sliced strawberries	625 mL
1/4 cup	confectioner's (icing) sugar	60 mL

1. Brush one side of each bread slice with butter. Place on a work surface, buttered side down.

2. In a small bowl, combine mascarpone and honey. Spread mascarpone mixture equally over bread slices. Top with strawberries and remaining bread slice and press together gently.

3. Place sandwiches on preheated panini grill or in a large skillet over medium-high heat and cook, turning once if using a skillet, for 3 to 4 minutes or until golden brown. Serve immediately and sift with confectioner's sugar.

Variation

Substitute four 8-inch (20 cm) tortilla wraps for the bread slices.

Pumpkin-Spiced Croissant

Serves 4

I couldn't decide if this should be in the Breakfast and Brunch or Dessert chapter. It's so good, it could go either place.

- **Panini grill or large skillet**
- **Preheat panini grill to medium, if using**

4	croissants, split and toasted	4
2 tbsp	butter, softened	30 mL
½ cup	Pumpkin Spice Cream Cheese (page 196) or store-bought	125 mL
½ cup	chopped pecans, toasted	125 mL

1. Brush outside of each croissant with butter. Place on a work surface, buttered side down. Spread cream cheese mixture equally over croissants. Sprinkle with pecans and top with remaining croissant half, buttered side up, pressing together gently.

2. Place sandwiches on preheated panini grill or in a large skillet over medium heat and cook, turning once if using a skillet, for 3 to 4 minutes or until golden brown and warmed. Serve immediately.

Variation

This recipe is also delicious on brioche bread and topped with walnuts and chopped dried dates or figs.

Mozzarella en Carozza

This Italian appetizer sandwich translates to "in a carriage," meaning the mozzarella is encased between two layers of firm sandwich bread and dipped in egg and fried. It is so delectable!

Tip

I typically use kosher or sea salt in my recipes, but feel free to use what you have on hand.

- **Panini grill or large skillet**
- **Preheat greased panini grill to medium, if using**

2	eggs	2
½ cup	milk	125 mL
½ tsp	kosher salt (see Tip, left)	2 mL
8	slices white bread (½-inch/1 cm thick slices)	8
8	slices mozzarella cheese	8

1. In a small bowl, whisk together eggs, milk and salt. Set aside.

2. Place bread slices on a work surface. Top with cheese slices. Press slices together gently to form 4 sandwiches. Dip sandwiches in egg mixture, one at a time, coating each side.

3. Place sandwiches on preheated panini grill or in a large skillet over medium heat and cook, turning once if using a skillet, for 3 to 4 minutes or until golden brown and cheese is melted. Serve immediately.

Variation

If you want a thicker bread for this rich sandwich, try challah bread.

Muenster-Stuffed Raisin Bread

Serves 4

This is one of my go-to recipes for the kids for breakfast, an afternoon snack or even dessert. Muenster is such a mild cheese and pairs perfectly with raisin bread and a touch of honey.

- **Panini grill or large skillet**
- **Preheat panini grill to medium, if using**

8	slices raisin bread ($\frac{1}{2}$-inch/1 cm thick slices)	8
2 tbsp	butter, softened	30 mL
$\frac{1}{4}$ cup	liquid honey	60 mL
8 oz	Muenster cheese, cut into 4 slices	250 g

1. Brush one side of each bread slice with butter. Place on a work surface, buttered sided down. Drizzle honey over 4 bread slices and top equally with Muenster cheese. Cover with remaining bread slices, buttered side up, and press together gently.

2. Place sandwiches on preheated panini grill or in a large skillet over medium heat and cook, turning once if using a skillet, for 3 to 4 minutes or until golden brown and cheese is melted. Serve immediately.

Variations

Feel free to substitute any of your favorite cheeses for Muenster.

If you're kids don't like raisins, purchase the cinnamon-swirl type bread.

Chocolate Hazelnut–Stuffed French Toast

Serves 4

Hazelnut spreads, such as Nutella, are made with hazelnuts, cocoa and skim milk. Combine it with Honey-Walnut Cream Cheese (page 195) for a wonderful stuffed French toast filling.

Tip

If the challah slices are very large, cut them in half for smaller sandwiches.

4	eggs, lightly beaten	4
1/4 cup	skim milk	60 mL
8	slices challah bread	8
4 tbsp	Honey-Walnut Cream Cheese, softened (page 195)	60 mL
4 tbsp	chocolate-hazelnut spread, such as Nutella	60 mL
2 tbsp	butter	30 mL
1/2 cup	honey or maple syrup, optional	125 mL

1. In a medium shallow bowl, combine eggs and milk.

2. Place bread slices on a work surface. Spread one side of each bread slice equally with Honey-Walnut Cream Cheese and chocolate-hazelnut spread. Cover with remaining bread slices, pressing together gently.

3. In a large skillet, melt butter over medium heat. Dip sandwiches in egg mixture to coat both sides. Cook sandwiches, turning once, for 3 to 5 minutes per side or until browned. Serve immediately with honey or syrup, if desired.

Variation

If you don't have a hazelnut spread on hand, use 4 oz (125 g) melted chocolate or any nut butter.

Breakfast Sausage Quesadillas

These breakfast quesadillas are great for a weekend hearty breakfast when you have company in town or just want something special and a little different.

Tip

If you use reduced-fat sausage, there is no need to drain. Then, you can omit the butter and use the same skillet. This reduces fat and cleanup.

12 oz	pork sausage (see Tip, left)	375 g
1 tbsp	butter	15 mL
10	large eggs, beaten	10
1½ cups	shredded pepper Jack cheese	375 mL
¼ tsp	salt	1 mL
⅛ tsp	freshly ground black pepper	0.5 mL
6	8-inch (20 cm) flour tortillas, warmed (see Tips, page 32)	6

Toppings, optional

Salsa

Sour cream

Avocado

Green onions

1. In a large nonstick skillet coated with cooking spray, cook sausage over medium-high heat for 10 minutes or until sausage crumbles and is no longer pink. Drain and pat dry with paper towels. Set aside.

2. In a large skillet, melt butter over medium heat. Add egg and cook for 3 minutes, stirring frequently to scrape bottom and sides of pan. Stir in sausage, cheese, salt and pepper and cook, stirring frequently, for 2 minutes or until cheese is melted.

3. Place tortillas on a work surface. Spoon sausage mixture equally over each tortilla. Fold in half, pressing gently to seal.

4. Coat a large skillet with cooking spray. Add tortillas and cook over medium heat in batches, for 3 minutes per side or until lightly browned and cheese is melted. Top with desired toppings and serve immediately.

Variation

If you like less spicy flavor, use Monterey Jack cheese instead of pepper Jack.

Grilled Huevos Rancheros

Serves 4

The first time I ever ate Huevos Rancheros was in Boulder, Colorado, while I was in college. It's rare to find them on a menu in Birmingham, and this recipe is definitely worth a try.

Tips

To warm tortillas: Place tortillas in the microwave on High for 10 seconds or warm over medium heat in a skillet for about 15 minutes.

Don't forget to drain and rinse canned beans to get rid of excess salt.

4	large eggs, lightly beaten	4
1/4 tsp	salt	1 mL
1/4 tsp	freshly ground black pepper	1 mL
1 tbsp	butter	15 mL
1	can (14 to 19 oz/398 to 540 mL) black beans, rinsed and drained	1
1	small tomato, sliced	1
1/3 cup	sliced black olives	75 mL
2 tbsp	chopped red onion	30 mL
1 cup	salsa or Pico de Gallo (page 180) or store-bought	250 mL
4	8-inch (20 cm) flour tortillas, warmed (see Tips, left)	4
1 cup	shredded Cheddar cheese	250 mL

Toppings, optional

Salsa

Sour cream

Sliced avocado

Freshly chopped cilantro

1. In a bowl, whisk together eggs, salt and pepper.

2. In a medium skillet, melt butter over medium heat. Add eggs and cook, stirring, for 3 to 4 minutes or until scrambled. Set aside.

3. In a large nonstick skillet over low heat, combine beans, tomato, olives and red onion. Stir in salsa and cook, stirring, for 5 to 10 minutes or until thickened.

4. Place tortillas on a work surface. Divide egg mixture equally in center of each tortilla. Arrange cheese equally over top and fold tortilla in half.

5. Coat a large skillet with cooking spray. Add tortillas and cook over medium heat, turning once, for 3 to 4 minutes or until golden brown and cheese is melted. Serve immediately with desired toppings.

Grilled Egg, Cheese and Bacon Biscuit

This has to be one of my three kids' favorite breakfast recipes in this book. It is definitely a family favorite.

- **Panini grill or large skillet**
- **Preheat panini grill to medium, if using**

4	large eggs, lightly beaten	4
1 tbsp	skim milk	15 mL
1/4 tsp	salt	1 mL
1/4 tsp	freshly ground black pepper	1 mL
6 tbsp	butter, divided	90 mL
4	biscuits, sliced	4
4	slices bacon, cooked and halved	4
1/4 cup	shredded Cheddar cheese	60 mL

1. In a medium bowl, combine eggs, milk, salt and pepper.

2. In a skillet, melt 1 tbsp (15 mL) of the butter over medium heat. Add egg mixture and cook, stirring, until scrambled. Set aside egg mixture and wipe skillet clean.

3. Spread remaining butter equally over biscuit tops. Place on a work surface, buttered side down. Top 4 halves equally with scrambled eggs, bacon, cheese and remaining biscuit half. Place biscuits, buttered side down, on preheated panini grill or in a skillet over medium heat and cook, turning once if using a skillet, for 3 to 5 minutes per side or until browned and cheese is melted. Serve immediately.

Variation

To make this lighter, use turkey bacon, 8 egg whites instead of 4 eggs and reduced-fat cheese.

Scrambled Egg Panini

My kids love making panini sandwiches for breakfast. This is always a crowd pleaser and an easy go-to recipe.

Tip

Check the stamped date on the package of bacon to make sure it's fresh.

• **Preheat panini grill or large skillet**

4	large eggs, lightly beaten	4
1 tbsp	milk	15 mL
1/4 tsp	salt	1 mL
1/4 tsp	freshly ground black pepper	1 mL
6 tbsp	butter, softened, divided	90 mL
8	slices whole wheat bread (1/2-inch/1 cm thick slices)	8
4	slices bacon, cooked	4
1/4 cup	shredded Cheddar cheese	60 mL

1. In a medium bowl, combine eggs, milk, salt and pepper.

2. In a skillet, melt 1 tbsp (15 mL) of the butter over medium heat. Add egg mixture and cook, stirring frequently, until scrambled. Set aside egg mixture and wipe skillet clean.

3. Place bread slices on a work surface. Spread remaining butter equally over bread slices. Place bread slices, buttered side down, on preheated panini grill or in a skillet over medium heat. Top with scrambled eggs, bacon, cheese and remaining bread slice. Cook, turning once if using a skillet, for 3 to 5 minutes per side or until browned and cheese is melted. Serve immediately.

Variations

Scrambled Egg and Fontina Panini: Omit Cheddar. Add 1 cup (250 mL) shredded Fontina cheese to the egg mixture and proceed as directed.

Wild Mushroom Cheddar Panini: Sauté $1^{1}/_{2}$ cups (375 mL) chopped wild mushrooms in 1 tbsp (15 mL) butter before adding eggs. Remove from skillet. Cook eggs until scrambled. Add mushrooms and proceed as directed.

To make this lighter, use 2 eggs and 3 egg whites. Omit the bacon and use 4 thinly sliced tomatoes instead.

Grilled Smoked Salmon Bagel

If you love smoked salmon in a bagel, you'll be addicted to this "grilled" version made with Garlic-Herb Cream Cheese (page 197).

Tip

Serve with capers, chives and red onion. This makes a great idea for a breakfast or brunch.

- **Panini grill or large skillet**
- **Preheat panini grill to medium, if using**

4	sesame, multigrain or other type bagels, split and toasted	4
2 tbsp	butter, softened	30 mL
½ cup	Garlic-Herb Cream Cheese (page 197) or store-bought	125 mL
8 oz	smoked salmon, cut into thin slices	250 mL
1	large tomato, thinly sliced	1
2 tbsp	chopped fresh basil	30 mL

1. Brush top half of each bagel slice with butter. Place on a work surface, buttered side down. Spread 4 bagel halves equally with cream cheese mixture. Top equally with smoked salmon, tomato and basil. Cover with remaining bagel halves, buttered side up, and press together gently.

2. Place sandwiches on preheated panini grill or in a large skillet over medium heat and cook, turning once if using a skillet, for 3 to 4 minutes or until golden brown and cheese is melted. Serve immediately.

Grilled Smoked Salmon and Brie

Serves 4

The saltiness of smoked salmon and buttery Brie make a wonderful gooey combination.

Tip

To keep Brie fresher longer, wrap it in parchment or wax paper and refrigerate.

- Panini grill or large skillet
- Preheat panini grill to medium, if using

8	slices sourdough bread (1/2-inch/1 cm thick slices)	8
2 tbsp	butter or margarine, softened	30 mL
4 oz	cream cheese, softened	125 g
8 oz	smoked salmon, cut into thin slices	250 g
4 oz	Brie, thinly sliced	125 g
1 cup	sliced red onions	250 mL

1. Brush one side of each bread slice with butter. Place on a work surface, buttered side down. Spread 4 bread slices equally with cream cheese. Top equally with smoked salmon, Brie and red onions. Cover with remaining bread slices, buttered side up, and press together gently.

2. Place sandwiches on preheated panini grill or in a large skillet over medium heat and cook, turning once if using a skillet, for 3 to 4 minutes or until golden brown and cheese is melted. Serve immediately.

Variation

If desired, substitute goat cheese for the Brie and 1 cup (250 mL) baby spinach leaves in this recipe.

Appetizers

Grilled Gruyère with Caramelized Onions

Makes 16

Caramelizing the onions flavors the Gruyère to perfection in this melt-in-your-mouth sandwich.

Tip

Caramelized onions are wonderful on an array of sandwiches and also great on pizza.

- **Panini grill or large skillet**
- **Preheat panini grill to medium, if using**

1 tbsp	unsalted butter	15 mL
1 tbsp	olive oil	15 mL
4 cups	sliced onions	1 L
1 tbsp	granulated sugar	15 mL
1/8 tsp	salt	0.5 mL
8	slices Italian bread (1/2-inch/1 cm thick slices)	8
1/4 cup	butter or margarine, softened	60 mL
1/4 cup	liquid honey	60 mL
4 oz	Gruyère cheese, thinly sliced	125 g

1. In a large skillet, melt 1 tbsp (15 mL) of the butter and oil over medium-low heat. Add onions, sugar and salt. Cover and sweat, stirring occasionally, for 20 minutes. Uncover and continue to cook, stirring frequently, for about 15 minutes or until onions are lightly browned.

2. Brush one side of each bread slice with butter. Place on a work surface, buttered side down. Spread 4 bread slices equally with honey. Top equally with cheese and onions. Cover with remaining bread slices, buttered side up, and press together gently.

3. Place sandwiches on preheated panini grill or in a large skillet over medium heat and cook, turning once if using a skillet, for 3 to 4 minutes or until golden brown and cheese is melted. Slice each sandwich into 4 slices for appetizer servings. Serve immediately.

Variation

Substitute Swiss cheese for the Gruyère cheese, if you like.

Caprese Panini

Makes 16

This twist on caprese salad makes a simple grilled cheese that everyone will love.

Tip

Purchase fresh mozzarella packed in water for best quality.

- **Panini grill or large skillet**
- **Preheat panini grill to medium, if using**

8	slices sourdough bread ($\frac{1}{2}$-inch/1 cm thick slices)	8
2 tbsp	olive oil	30 mL
2	tomatoes, thinly sliced	2
4 oz	fresh mozzarella, sliced into 4 slices (see Tip, left)	125 g
$\frac{1}{2}$ cup	fresh basil leaves	125 mL
	Balsamic vinegar, optional	

1. Brush one side of each bread slice with olive oil. Place on a work surface, oiled side down. Top 4 bread slices equally with tomatoes, mozzarella slices and basil. Cover with remaining bread slices, oiled side up, and press together gently.

2. Place sandwiches on preheated panini grill or in a large skillet over medium heat and cook, turning once if using a skillet, for 3 to 4 minutes or until golden brown and cheese is melted. Drizzle with balsamic vinegar, if desired. Slice each sandwich into 4 slices for appetizer servings. Serve immediately.

Grilled Brie with Chutney

This recipe was inspired by a foodie friend of mine, Kelley, in Utah. It makes use of two wonderful combinations: Brie and mango chutney. I made these sandwiches for a shower party and everyone loved them.

Tip

To add more protein to this sandwich, add sliced grilled chicken or turkey.

- **Panini grill or large skillet**
- **Preheat panini grill to medium, if using**

8	slices pumpernickel bread (½-inch/1 cm thick slices)	8
2 tbsp	butter or margarine, softened	30 mL
¼ cup	liquid honey	60 mL
4 oz	Brie, thinly sliced	125 g
1 cup	baby spinach leaves	250 mL
1½ cups	Peach-Ginger Chutney (page 176)	375 mL

1. Brush one side of each bread slice with butter. Place on a work surface, buttered side down. Spread 4 bread slices equally with honey. Top equally with Brie, spinach leaves and chutney. Cover with remaining bread slices, buttered side up, and press together gently.

2. Place sandwiches on preheated panini grill or in a large skillet over medium heat and cook, turning once if using a skillet, for 3 to 4 minutes or until golden brown and cheese is melted. Slice each sandwich into 4 slices for appetizer servings. Serve immediately.

Variations

Substitute the Peach-Ginger Chutney with either Mango Chutney (page 176) or Plum Chutney (Variation, page 176).

Grilled Cheese and Cherry Tomato Relish

Makes 16		

Cherry tomatoes are the star of this grilled cheese sandwich filled with Italian flair.

Tip

Grate a large wedge of Parmesan and then refrigerate it in an airtight container to use as needed. If you're short on time, purchase already grated Parmesan.

- **Panini grill or large skillet**
- **Preheat panini grill to medium, if using**

8	slices Italian bread ($\frac{1}{2}$-inch/1 cm thick slices)	8
$\frac{1}{4}$ cup	butter or margarine, softened	60 mL
$\frac{1}{4}$ cup	Basil Pesto (page 181) or store-bought	60 mL
4	slices mozzarella cheese	4
$\frac{1}{2}$ cup	freshly grated Parmesan cheese (see Tip, left)	125 mL
1 cup	fresh spinach leaves	250 mL
$1\frac{1}{3}$ cups	Cherry Tomato Relish (page 178)	325 mL

1. Brush one side of each bread slice with butter. Place on a work surface, buttered side down. Spread 4 bread slices equally with Basil Pesto. Top equally with mozzarella and Parmesan cheeses, spinach and Cherry Tomato Relish. Cover with remaining bread slices, buttered side up, and press together gently.

2. Place sandwiches on preheated panini grill or in a large skillet over medium heat and cook, turning once if using a skillet, for 3 to 4 minutes or until golden brown and cheese is melted. Slice each sandwich into 4 slices for appetizer servings. Serve immediately.

Grilled Olive Caponata and Goat Cheese

Makes 16

I love cooking with olives and goat cheese. When these two ingredients are melted together in a sandwich, it tastes even better.

Tip

Goat cheese is often labeled as "chèvre" and is sold in a variety of sizes and shapes, such as logs and cones.

- **Panini grill or large skillet**
- **Preheat panini grill to medium, if using**

8	slices sourdough bread (½-inch/1 cm thick slices)	8
2 tbsp	olive oil	30 mL
½ cup	Caponata Spread (page 187) or store-bought	125 mL
½ cup	fresh basil leaves	125 mL
4 oz	crumbled goat cheese (see Tip, left)	125 g
	Balsamic vinegar, optional	

1. Brush one side of each bread slice with olive oil. Place on a work surface, oiled side down. Spread caponata equally over bread slices. Top 4 slices equally with basil and goat cheese. Cover with remaining bread slices, oiled side up, and press together gently.

2. Place sandwiches on preheated panini grill or in a large skillet over medium heat and cook, turning once if using a skillet, for 3 to 4 minutes or until golden brown and cheese is melted. Drizzle with balsamic vinegar, if desired. Slice each sandwich into 4 slices for appetizer servings. Serve immediately.

Grilled Brie, Apple and Thyme

Makes 16

This combination of Brie, apples and fresh thyme can't be beat. It's the perfect fall lunch or appetizer sandwich.

- Panini grill or large skillet
- Preheat panini grill to medium, if using

¼ cup	liquid honey	60 mL
1 tbsp	finely chopped fresh thyme	15 mL
8	slices raisin bread (½-inch/1 cm thick slices)	8
2 tbsp	butter or margarine, softened	30 mL
1	apple, such as Fuji, Braeburn or Gala, thinly sliced	1
4 oz	Brie, thinly sliced	125 g

1. In a small bowl, combine honey and thyme.

2. Brush one side of each bread slice with butter. Place on a work surface, buttered side down. Spread 4 bread slices equally with honey mixture. Top equally with apple and Brie. Cover with remaining bread slices, buttered side up, and press together gently.

3. Place sandwiches on preheated panini grill or in a large skillet over medium heat and cook, turning once if using a skillet, for 3 to 4 minutes or until golden brown and cheese is melted. Slice each sandwich into 4 slices for appetizer servings. Serve immediately.

Variation

I love to substitute fresh sliced plums for the apples in this recipe.

Grilled Peaches, Mozzarella and Peach Salsa

This summertime favorite is perfect in July or August when peaches are at their peak. Feel free to substitute turkey, roast beef or prosciutto for the ham, or omit the deli meat altogether.

Tip

Choose peaches that are fragrant and give slightly to palm pressure. Store ripe peaches in a plastic bag for up to 5 days. Store unripe fruit at room temperature.

- **Panini grill or large skillet**
- **Preheat panini grill to medium, if using**

8	slices sourdough bread (1/2-inch/1 cm thick slices)	8
2 tbsp	butter or margarine, softened	30 mL
1/4 cup	liquid honey	60 mL
12 oz	thinly sliced ham	375 g
1 cup	thinly sliced peaches (see Tip, left)	250 mL
8	slices mozzarella cheese	8
1 cup	Peach Salsa (page 179)	250 mL

1. Brush one side of each bread slice with butter. Place on a work surface, buttered side down. Spread 4 bread slices equally with honey. Top with ham, peaches, cheese and Peach Salsa. Cover with remaining bread slices, buttered side up, and press together gently.

2. Place sandwiches on preheated panini grill or in a large skillet over medium heat and cook, turning once if using a skillet, for 3 to 4 minutes or until golden brown and cheese is melted. Slice each sandwich into 4 slices for appetizer servings. Serve immediately.

Variation

Goat cheese also works great instead of the mozzarella.

Grilled Peach and Brie

Makes 16

I make these very often in the summertime. It's a top request at my house.

Tip

Use leftover chives in salads, chicken dishes and any recipe in which you might want to replace the onions.

- **Panini grill or large skillet**
- **Preheat panini grill to medium, if using**

8	slices multigrain, country whole wheat or oat bread (1/2-inch/1 cm thick slices)	8
2 tbsp	butter or margarine, softened	30 mL
2 tbsp	liquid honey	30 mL
3/4 cup	baby spinach leaves	175 mL
2	large peaches, thinly sliced	2
5 oz	Brie, thinly sliced	150 g
2 tbsp	chopped fresh chives	30 mL

1. Brush one side of each bread slice with butter. Place on a work surface, buttered side down. Spread honey equally over 4 slices. Top equally with spinach, peaches, Brie and chives. Cover with remaining bread slices, buttered side up, and press together gently.

2. Place sandwiches on preheated panini grill or in a large skillet over medium heat and cook, turning once if using a skillet, for 3 to 4 minutes or until golden brown and cheese is melted. Slice each sandwich into 4 slices for appetizer servings. Serve immediately.

Prosciutto and Melon Grilled Cheese

Makes 16

This is a twist on a one of my favorite appetizers: prosciutto and melon. I turned it into a grilled cheese with a touch of Havarti, and now it's better than ever.

- Panini grill or large skillet
- Preheat panini grill to medium, if using

8	slices sourdough bread (½-inch/1 cm thick slices)	8
¼ cup	olive oil	60 mL
4 tsp	liquid honey	20 mL
12 oz	thinly sliced prosciutto	375 mL
1 cup	thinly sliced honeydew melon	250 mL
4	slices Havarti cheese	4
4 tsp	balsamic vinegar	20 mL

1. Brush one side of each bread slice with olive oil. Place on a work surface, oiled side down. Spread 4 bread slices equally with honey. Top equally with prosciutto, melon slices and Havarti. Drizzle equally with balsamic vinegar. Cover with remaining bread slices, oiled side up, and press together gently.

2. Place sandwiches on preheated panini grill or in a large skillet over medium heat and cook, turning once if using a skillet, for 3 to 4 minutes or until golden brown and cheese is melted. Slice each sandwich into 4 slices for appetizer servings. Serve immediately.

Grilled Prosciutto, Cantaloupe and Fontina

Makes 16

My friend and fellow foodie, Kelley, from Park City, Utah, gave me this idea. She told me it's her favorite summertime grilled cheese.

Tip

To pick a cantaloupe, look for one with a fresh melon odor, that is heavy for its size and yields slightly to pressure.

- Panini grill or large skillet
- Preheat panini grill to medium, if using

8	slices multigrain bread (1/2-inch/1 cm thick slices)	8
1/4 cup	butter or margarine, softened	60 mL
1/4 cup	honey mustard	60 mL
8 oz	thinly sliced prosciutto	250 g
1 cup	arugula or spinach leaves	250 mL
1/2	small cantaloupe, thinly sliced (see Tip, left)	1/2
4	slices fontina cheese	4

1. Brush one side of each bread slice with butter. Place on a work surface, buttered side down. Spread 4 bread slices equally with honey mustard. Top equally with prosciutto, arugula, cantaloupe and cheese. Cover with remaining bread slices, buttered side up, and press together gently.

2. Place sandwiches on preheated panini grill or in a large skillet over medium heat and cook, turning once if using a skillet, for 3 to 4 minutes or until golden brown and cheese is melted. Slice each sandwich into 4 slices for appetizer servings. Serve immediately.

Pear, Pecan and Gorgonzola Sandwich

I love to make these appetizer sandwiches in the fall. Pecans, pears and Gorgonzola make a fresh, flavorful autumn combination. Feel free to use gluten-free bread, if desired.

Tips

When purchasing pears, look for ones that are fragrant and have no blemishes. I store mine in the refrigerator in a plastic bag.

Store honey in a cool place away from direct sunlight in a tightly covered container. It is not necessary to refrigerate.

- Panini grill or large skillet
- Preheat panini grill to medium, if using

8	slices multigrain bread (1/2-inch/1 cm thick slices)	8
2 tbsp	butter or margarine, softened	30 mL
4 oz	cream cheese, softened	125 g
1/4 cup	crumbled Gorgonzola cheese	60 mL
1 1/2 cups	thinly sliced pears (about 2 medium) (see Tips, left)	375 mL
4 tbsp	liquid honey (see Tips, left)	60 mL
1/2 cup	chopped pecans, toasted (see Tips, page 25)	125 mL

1. Brush one side of each bread slice with butter. Place bread on a work surface, buttered side down.

2. In a small bowl, combine cream cheese and Gorgonzola. Spread each bread slices with 1 tbsp (15 mL) of the Gorgonzola mixture. Top 4 slices with pear slices. Drizzle with honey and sprinkle with pecans. Cover with remaining bread slices, buttered side up, and press together gently.

3. Place sandwiches on preheated panini grill or in a large skillet over medium heat, and cook, turning once if using a skillet, for 3 to 4 minutes or until golden brown and cheese is melted. Slice each sandwich into 4 slices for appetizer servings. Serve immediately.

Variation

You can also make these into regular-size sandwiches for a light lunch.

Havarti and Cucumber Sandwich

Makes 16

Havarti is a buttery, semisoft cheese from Denmark. It pairs nicely with homemade Garlic-Herb Cream Cheese and sliced cucumber.

Tips

If you can find Havarti with dill, use that for extra dill flavor.

You can also make these into regular sandwiches for a light lunch served with a tossed salad or cup of soup.

Feel free to use gluten-free bread for a gluten-free recipe.

- **Panini grill or large skillet**
- **Preheat panini grill to medium, if using**

8	slices Italian bread (about ½-inch/1 cm thick slices)	8
2 tbsp	olive oil	30 mL
½ cup	Garlic-Herb Cream Cheese (page 197) or store-bought vegetable cream cheese	125 mL
¾ cup	thinly sliced cucumber	175 mL
4 oz	Havarti, thinly sliced	125 g
2 tbsp	chopped fresh dill, optional	30 mL

1. Brush one side of each bread slice with olive oil. Place bread on a work surface, oiled side down.

2. Spread each bread slice with 1 tbsp (15 mL) of the cream cheese mixture. Top 2 slices equally with cucumber and cheese. Top with dill, if desired. Cover with remaining bread slices, oiled side up, and press together gently.

3. Place sandwiches on preheated panini grill or in a large skillet over medium heat, and cook, turning once if using a skillet, for 3 to 4 minutes or until golden brown and cheese is melted. Slice each sandwich into 4 slices for appetizer servings. Serve immediately.

Roast Beef with Asiago and Watercress

The rich, nutty flavor of Asiago makes the perfect flavor profile with the roast beef and watercress. I love to serve these for a simple dinner.

- Panini grill or large skillet
- Preheat panini grill to medium, if using

8	slices whole-grain bread (½-inch/1 cm thick slices)	8
¼ cup	butter or margarine, softened	60 mL
¼ cup	Dijon mustard	60 mL
12 oz	sliced roast beef	375 g
1 cup	watercress leaves	250 mL
4 oz	Asiago cheese, thinly sliced	125 g

1. Brush one side of each bread slice with butter. Place on a work surface, buttered side down. Spread 4 bread slices equally with mustard. Top equally with roast beef, watercress and cheese. Cover with remaining bread slices, buttered side up, and press gently.

2. Place sandwiches on preheated panini grill or in a large skillet over medium heat and cook, turning once if using a skillet, for 3 to 4 minutes or until golden brown and cheese is melted. Slice each sandwich into 4 slices for appetizer servings. Serve immediately.

Variation

Feel free to substitute mixed lettuce for the watercress.

Grilled Four-Cheese Minis

Makes about 16

This classic grilled cheese is made with four cheeses and preserves. Feel free to use any of your favorite type of preserves and cheeses to create your own.

Tip

Sandwich round thins are made by many major bread companies and are packed in bags and usually found in the bread section of the grocery store. They are also sold in mini versions, perfect if you halve this recipe.

- **Panini grill or large skillet**
- **Preheat panini grill to medium, if using**

8	slices sandwich round thins or sourdough bread (1/2-inch/ 1 cm thick slices)	8
2 tbsp	butter, softened	30 mL
1/4 cup	blackberry preserves or jam	60 mL
2 oz	Cheddar slices	60 g
2 oz	Muenster slices	60 g
2 oz	Swiss slices	60 g
2 oz	white Cheddar cheese slices	60 g

1. Brush one side of each bread slice with butter. Place on a work surface, buttered sided down. Spread bread slices equally with preserves. Top 4 slices with Cheddar, Muenster, Swiss and white Cheddar cheeses. Cover with top halves of bread, buttered side up, and press together gently.

2. Place sandwiches on preheated panini grill or in a large skillet over medium heat and cook, turning once if using a skillet, for 3 to 4 minutes or until golden brown and cheese is melted. Cut into mini slices and serve immediately.

Variations

Substitute whole-grain bread for the sourdough and use apricot, peach or strawberry preserves, if you can't find blackberry.

Three-Cheese Grilled Sliders with Compound Herb Butter

Makes 8

Impress your guests by making this upscale version of the classic grilled cheese. The aromas from the compound herb butter create a sandwich sure to please.

Tip

You can use compound butter on crostini or as a topping on meats and seafood. If you have leftover compound butter, shape it into a log and refrigerate or freeze it. It will keep in the refrigerator for up to 2 days or in the freezer for 2 weeks.

- Panini grill or large skillet
- Preheat panini grill to medium, if using

Compound Herb Butter

1 cup	unsalted butter, at room temperature	250 mL
1	clove garlic, minced	1
1 tbsp	chopped fresh chives	15 mL
1 tbsp	chopped fresh rosemary	15 mL
1 tbsp	chopped fresh thyme, minced	15 mL
16	slices sourdough baguette (1-inch/2.5 cm thick slices)	16
1 oz	fontina cheese, thinly sliced	30 g
2 oz	mozzarella cheese, thinly sliced	60 g
2 oz	Gruyère cheese, thinly sliced	60 g

1. *Compound Herb Butter:* In a small bowl, whisk together butter, garlic, chives, rosemary and thyme until combined.

2. Spread about 1 tbsp (15 mL) of the herb butter on one side of each bread slice. Place on a work surface, buttered side down. Top 8 slices equally with fontina, mozzarella and Gruyère cheeses. Cover with remaining bread slices, buttered side up, and press together gently.

3. Place sandwiches on preheated panini grill or in a large skillet over medium heat and cook, turning once if using a skillet, for 3 to 4 minutes or until golden brown and cheese is melted. Serve immediately.

Variation

If you are unable to find Gruyère cheese, substitute with a hard Swiss cheese.

Grilled Cheese Sliders with Caramelized Balsamic Onions

The traditional grilled cheese is taken to the next level by the addition of caramelized balsamic onions. This recipe was developed by my friend, Jessica, of thenovicechefblog.com.

• **Panini grill or large skillet**
• **Preheat panini grill to medium, if using**

4 tbsp	unsalted butter, softened divided	60 mL
1	small yellow onion, thinly sliced	1
¼ cup	balsamic vinegar	60 mL
1 tbsp	granulated sugar	15 mL
½ tsp	salt	2 mL
¼ tsp	freshly ground black pepper	1 mL
16	slices sourdough baguette (1-inch/2.5 cm thick slices)	16
3 oz	fontina cheese, thinly sliced	90 g
2 oz	mozzarella cheese, thinly sliced	60 g

1. In a medium skillet, melt 1 tbsp (15 mL) of the butter over medium-low heat. Add onion and cook, without stirring, for 10 to 15 minutes or until onion begins to develop a deep caramel color. Add balsamic vinegar, sugar, salt and pepper. Cook, stirring occasionally, for 10 minutes or until onion mixture thickens. Remove from heat and set aside.

2. Spread remaining butter on one side of each bread slice. Place on a work surface, buttered side down. Top 8 slices equally with fontina, mozzarella and balsamic caramelized onions. Cover with remaining bread slices, buttered side up, and press together gently.

3. Place sandwiches on preheated panini grill or in a large skillet over medium heat and cook, turning once if using a skillet, for 3 to 4 minutes or until golden brown and cheese is melted. Serve immediately.

Variation

If you can't find fontina cheese, substitute provolone.

Italian Tomato–Basil Bread

Makes about 12

This easy appetizer is one of my kids' favorites. It's so good that you must be cautious not to fill up on this before dinner (speaking from experience).

• **Preheat broiler with rack 4 inches (10 cm) from heat**

1	loaf (1 lb/500 g) French bread, sliced diagonally into 1-inch (2.5 cm) thick slices	1
1/4 cup	olive oil	60 mL
8	Roma (plum) tomatoes, thinly sliced	8
1/2 cup	oil-packed sun-dried tomatoes	125 mL
2 tbsp	chopped fresh basil	30 mL
4 oz	freshly shaved Parmesan cheese	125 g

1. Arrange baguette slices on a large baking sheet. Brush each side of bread slice with olive oil. Bake in preheated oven for 5 minutes or until lightly toasted. Let stand for 5 minutes. Top equally with tomatoes, sun-dried tomatoes, basil and cheese. Reduce oven temperature to 375°F (190°C) and toast again until cheese is melted. Serve immediately.

Variation

Add toasted pine nuts after you top with basil and then the cheese.

Hot Bacon Swiss Crostini

**Makes
8 to 10**

*Everyone in the south
loves a bacon appetizer.
The addition of nonfat
Greek yogurt is the
secret ingredient to
make it creamier and
healthier.*

Tip

This dip makes a great
party appetizer with or
without the crostini.
It also saves well for
leftovers. Store in an
airtight container in the
refrigerator for up to
3 days.

- **Preheat oven to 350°F (180°C)**
- **8-inch (20 cm) square metal baking pan or
  glass baking dish, lightly greased**

1	package (8 oz/250 g) cream cheese, softened	1
1/4 cup	plain nonfat Greek yogurt	60 mL
1/4 cup	reduced-fat mayonnaise	60 mL
8 oz	white Cheddar cheese, shredded	250 g
3	green onions, white parts and a bit of green, chopped	3
8	slices bacon, cooked and crumbled	8
1/2 cup	crushed buttery crackers	125 mL
8 to 10	baguette slices (about 1/2-inch/1 cm thick)	8 to 10
1/2 cup	finely chopped fresh Italian flat-leaf parsley	125 mL

1. In a large bowl, combine cream cheese, yogurt, mayonnaise, cheese and green onions. Spoon into prepared pan. Bake in preheated oven for 15 minutes. Turn oven to broil and heat for 2 more minutes, until slightly browned. Top with bacon and cracker crumbs.

2. Arrange baguette slices on a large baking sheet. Bake in preheated oven for 5 minutes or until lightly toasted. Top equally with cheese mixture. Return to oven and bake for 5 more minutes or until browned. Sprinkle with parsley and serve immediately.

BLT Basil Crostini

BLT is an American classic. These ingredients also work well on this crostini recipe laced with a homemade Greek yogurt spread.

Tip

To lighten this recipe, use reduced-fat mayonnaise, nonfat Greek yogurt, turkey bacon and reduced-fat Swiss cheese.

- Preheat oven to 350°F (180°C)
- Preheat broiler with rack 4 inches (10 cm) from heat

8 to 10	French baguette slices (about ½-inch/1 cm thick slices)	8 to 10
¼ cup	mayonnaise	60 mL
¼ cup	plain Greek yogurt	60 mL
1 tsp	Dijon mustard	5 mL
½ tsp	freshly squeezed lemon juice	2 mL
1 tbsp	chopped fresh Italian flat-leaf parsley	15 mL
1 tbsp	chopped fresh basil (approx.)	15 mL
4	slices bacon, cooked and crumbled	4
3	Roma (plum) tomatoes, thinly sliced	3
1 cup	shredded Swiss cheese	250 mL

1. Arrange baguette slices on a large baking sheet. Bake in preheated oven for 5 minutes or until lightly toasted.

2. In a medium bowl, combine mayonnaise, yogurt, Dijon mustard, lemon juice, parsley and basil.

3. Spread mayonnaise mixture equally over bread rounds. Top with crumbled bacon, tomatoes and shredded cheese. Broil crostini for 2 minutes or until cheese is melted. Serve immediately and top with additional basil, if desired.

Variation

BLT Rounds: Cut any type of bread into 2½-inch (6 cm) slices with a biscuit cutter. Toast in a nonstick stick skillet or broiler pan for 2 minutes. Add toppings and proceed with directions above.

Crab and Goat Cheese Crostini

Makes 10 to 12

This appetizer with crab, fresh herbs, goat cheese and roasted red peppers is perfect for holidays. The crab really shines through when the crostini are heated.

Tip

Serve as an appetizer with steak, chicken, pasta or seafood.

● **Preheat oven to 400°F (200°C)**

8 oz	goat cheese, crumbled	250 g
1	garlic clove, minced	1
1 tbsp	chopped fresh rosemary	15 mL
1 tbsp	chopped fresh chives	15 mL
1/8 tsp	freshly ground black pepper	0.5 mL
1/2 cup	fresh crabmeat (about 4 oz/125 g)	125 mL
1/3 cup	diced roasted bell peppers	75 mL
24	slices French bread baguette (1-inch/2.5 cm thick slices)	24
	Chopped fresh chives, optional	

1. In a food processor or large bowl, combine goat cheese, garlic, rosemary, chives and pepper. Stir in crabmeat and red peppers.

2. Arrange baguette slices on a large baking sheet. Bake in preheated oven for 5 minutes or until lightly toasted. Spread crab mixture equally over bread slices and return to oven for 5 minutes until thoroughly heated and cheese is slightly melted. Top with chives, if desired, and serve immediately.

Light and Healthy

Grilled Cheese and Peach-Ginger Chutney

Serves 4

The ginger in the chutney adds a boost of flavor and punch. This is great to serve for a summertime lunch.

- Panini grill or large skillet
- Preheat panini grill to medium, if using

8	slices multigrain bread (1/2-inch/1 cm thick slices)	8
2 tbsp	butter or margarine, softened	30 mL
1/4 cup	liquid honey	60 mL
12 oz	thinly sliced turkey	375 g
2	peaches, thinly sliced (see Tip, page 46)	2
4 oz	part-skim mozzarella cheese, cut into 4 slices	125 g
1 cup	Peach-Ginger Chutney (page 176)	250 mL

1. Brush one side of each bread slice with butter. Place on a work surface, buttered side down. Spread 4 bread slices equally with honey. Top with turkey, peach slices, cheese and Peach-Ginger Chutney. Cover with remaining bread slices, buttered side up, and press together gently.

2. Place sandwiches on preheated panini grill or in a large skillet over medium heat and cook, turning once if using a skillet, for 3 to 4 minutes or until golden brown and cheese is melted. Serve immediately.

Lean Ham and Cheese Sandwich

Serves 4

Low-fat ham and cheese? Yes, it's possible with this twist using white Cheddar and a sweet and savory mixture of apricot preserves and cream cheese.

Tip

Let cream cheese soften slightly so it's easier to spread.

- **Panini grill or large skillet**
- **Preheat panini grill to medium, if using**

2 tbsp	apricot preserves or jam	30 mL
2 tbsp	reduced-fat cream cheese, softened	30 mL
8	slices whole wheat bread	8
4 tsp	butter, melted	20 mL
4 oz	lean ham	125 g
4	slices white Cheddar cheese	4

1. In a small bowl, combine preserves and cream cheese.

2. Brush one side of each bread slice with butter. Place on a work surface, buttered side down. Spread apricot mixture equally over each bread slice. Top 4 bread slices with ham and cheese. Cover with remaining bread slices, buttered side up, and press together gently.

3. Place sandwiches on preheated panini grill or in a large skillet over medium heat and cook, turning once if using a skillet, for 2 minutes per side or until cheese is melted. Serve immediately.

Variation

Substitute any of your favorite lean deli meats for the ham.

Healthy Deli Meats

- When selecting deli meats look at the fat content by reading the labels.
- Watch for high levels of sodium particularly in bacon, sausage and salami. Some brands have reduced-sodium versions.
- Look for deli meats that are free of MSG, artificial colors, flavors and preservatives, such as nitrites.
- Check the vegetarian section at your grocery store for vegetarian versions of meats.

Grilled Pepper Jack, Arugula and Sprouts

Serves 4

This healthy vegetarian sandwich is a breeze to prepare. It's made with the freshest ingredients including avocados, arugula, tomatoes and sprouts.

Tips

You can usually find "sprouted bread" in the freezer section of the grocery store.

To speed the ripening of avocados, place them in a paper bag with an apple. Pierce the bag in several places and store at room temperature for up to 3 days.

- **Panini grill or large skillet**
- **Preheat panini grill to medium, if using**

8	slices gluten-free or sprouted grain bread (1/2-inch/1 cm thick slices) (see Tips, left)	8
2 tbsp	butter, softened	30 mL
3/4 cup	Hummus (page 185) or store-bought	175 mL
4	slices pepper Jack cheese	4
2	avocados, thinly sliced (see Tips, left)	2
1/2 cup	arugula leaves	125 mL
1/2 cup	sliced tomatoes	125 mL
1/2 cup	alfalfa sprouts	125 mL
1/8 tsp	freshly ground black pepper	0.5 mL

1. Brush one side of each bread slice with butter. Place on a work surface, buttered side down. Spread 4 bread slices equally with hummus. Top equally with cheese, avocados, arugula, tomato slices and sprouts. Sprinkle with pepper. Cover with remaining bread slices, buttered side up, and press together gently.

2. Place sandwiches on a preheated panini grill or in a large skillet over medium heat and cook, turning once if using a skillet, for 3 to 4 minutes or until golden brown and cheese is melted. Serve immediately.

Grilled Goat Cheese and Figs (page 20)

Grilled Egg, Cheese and Bacon Biscuit (page 33)

Prosciutto and Melon Grilled Cheese (page 48)

Healthy Pan Bagnat Grilled Cheese (page 65)

Classic Grilled Two Cheese (page 80)

Grilled Guacomento (page 81)

Grilled Roast Beef and Stilton (page 101)

Grilled Carnegie Sandwich (page 109)

Chicken, Apple and Smoked Gouda (page 114)

Healthy Pan Bagnat Grilled Cheese

Serves 4

Pan bagnat is a name for a sandwich originating from Nice, France, that consists of ingredients in a Salade Niçoise. This is a twist without the hard-boiled eggs.

Tip

If you don't have sherry vinegar, you can substitute red wine or white wine vinegar.

- Panini grill or large skillet
- Preheat panini grill to medium, if using

2 tbsp	sherry vinegar (see Tip, left)	30 mL
2 tsp	freshly squeezed lemon juice	10 mL
7 tsp	olive oil, divided	35 mL
¼ tsp	freshly ground black pepper	1 mL
2	cans (each 7 oz/210 g) solid white tuna, packed in water, drained	2
1 tbsp	finely chopped red onion	15 mL
1 tbsp	chopped fresh basil	15 mL
8	slices sprouted or whole-grain bread (½-inch/1 cm thick slices)	8
4	Roma (plum) tomatoes, thinly sliced	4
1 cup	baby spinach leaves	250 mL
4 oz	shaved Parmesan cheese	125 g

1. In small bowl, whisk together vinegar, lemon juice, 1 tsp (5 mL) of the olive oil and pepper.

2. In a medium bowl, combine tuna, red onion and basil. Stir in sherry mixture, mixing well.

3. Brush one side of each bread slice with remaining oil. Place on a work surface, oiled side down. Top 4 bread slices equally with tuna mixture, tomato, spinach and cheese. Cover with remaining bread slices, oiled side up, and press together gently.

4. Place sandwiches on a preheated panini grill or in a large skillet over medium heat and cook, turning once if using a skillet, for 3 to 4 minutes or until golden brown and cheese is melted. Serve immediately.

Open-Faced Couscous Chicken Salad with Goat Cheese

I like to use rotisserie chicken purchased from the grocery store to make this recipe even easier.

Tip

To prepare couscous, follow package directions. Couscous can be found in the rice section of the grocery store.

• **Preheat broiler with rack 4 inches (10 cm) from heat**

2 cups	chopped cooked chicken	500 mL
1½ cups	cooked couscous (see Tip, left)	375 mL
1½ cups	halved grape tomatoes	375 mL
½ cup	chopped fresh basil	125 mL
¼ cup	sherry or balsamic vinegar	60 mL
2 tbsp	olive oil	30 mL
¼ tsp	freshly ground black pepper	1 mL
4	slices multigrain bread (½-inch/1 cm thick slices)	4
4 oz	crumbled goat cheese	125 g

1. In a large bowl, combine chicken, couscous, tomatoes, basil, vinegar, oil and pepper. Spoon mixture equally over bread slices and top equally with goat cheese. Place on a large baking sheet.

2. Broil for 2 minutes or until cheese is melted. Serve immediately.

Broiling versus Grilling

Sometimes using your broiler when making grilled cheese sandwiches can have its advantages, especially in light cooking. You most likely will use less butter or oil when you're broiling. It's also a great way to make open-faced sandwiches and cleanup is a snap.

Open-Faced Spinach and Havarti

This healthy sandwich is filling and so fresh.

Tip

You can find Havarti with dill in the specialty cheese section of your grocery store or in specialty cheese shops. If you can't find it, use regular Havarti or part-skim mozzarella cheese.

• **Preheat broiler with rack 4 inches (10 cm) from heat**

1 tbsp	olive oil	15 mL
4 cups	baby spinach	1 L
4	whole wheat English muffins, split and toasted	4
½ cup	Garlic-Herb Cream Cheese (page 197) or store-bought	125 mL
2	Roma (plum) tomatoes, thinly sliced	2
4	slices Havarti with dill (see Tip, left)	4

1. In a skillet, heat oil over medium heat. Add baby spinach and cook until slightly wilted.

2. Spread 1 tbsp (15 mL) Garlic-Herb Cream Cheese on each toasted English muffin half. Top halves equally with spinach, tomatoes and cheese. Place English muffin halves on a large baking sheet. Broil for 2 minutes or until cheese is melted. Serve immediately.

Variation

Use Sun-Dried Tomato Pesto (page 182) instead of the Garlic-Herb Cream Cheese.

Open-Faced Grilled Balsamic Chicken and Portobello

Balsamic vinegar, fresh rosemary and thyme make an easy, flavorful marinade for the chicken in this hearty sandwich.

Tip

Sliced baby bella mushrooms can be found in most grocery stores where fresh mushrooms are sold. If you can't find them, you can substitute sliced fresh button mushrooms.

- Preheat grill or oven to 400°F (200°C)
- Baking sheet, sprayed with cooking spray
- Grill or grill pan

1 lb	boneless skinless chicken cutlets	500 g
¼ cup + 2 tbsp	balsamic vinegar, divided	90 mL
1 tbsp	chopped fresh rosemary	15 mL
1 tbsp	chopped fresh thyme	15 mL
1 cup	baby bella mushrooms	125 mL
1 tbsp	olive oil	15 mL
4	(3 oz/90 g) whole wheat focaccia (each about 4 inches/ 10 cm), sliced horizontally	4
6 oz	part-skim mozzarella cheese, thinly sliced	175 mL
¾ cup	chopped fresh basil, optional	175 mL

1. In a shallow dish or resealable plastic bag, combine chicken, ¼ cup (60 mL) of the balsamic vinegar, rosemary and thyme. Cover or seal and marinate in the refrigerator for at least 1 hour or for up to 8 hours. Place chicken on a prepared baking sheet or grill pan, discarding marinade. Toss mushrooms in remaining 2 tbsp (30 mL) of balsamic vinegar

2. On a grill rack or grill pan, cook chicken for 4 to 6 minutes on each side or until lightly browned and no longer pink inside. Place mushrooms on grill or in the oven during the last 2 minutes of cooking.

3. Preheat oven to broil.

4. Place focaccia slices on a work surface. Top equally with chicken, mushrooms and cheese. Place open-faced on a baking sheet and broil for 1 to 2 minutes or until cheese is melted. Top with basil, if desired, and serve immediately.

Warm Peanut Butter Power Wrap

My kids went wild over this recipe. They love it for lunch and a hearty afternoon snack.

Tip

If you don't have time to make the Honey-Walnut Cream Cheese, you can use any store-bought flavored cream cheese and add 4 tsp (20 mL) liquid honey.

• **Large nonstick skillet, sprayed with cooking spray**

¼ cup	natural peanut butter	60 mL
¼ cup	Honey-Walnut Cream Cheese (page 195) or store-bought regular cream cheese, softened (see Tip, left)	60 mL
4	8-inch (20 cm) whole wheat wraps	4
2	bananas, sliced	2

1. In a small bowl, combine peanut butter and Honey-Walnut Cream Cheese.

2. Place tortillas on a work surface. Spread cream cheese mixture equally over each tortilla, leaving a 1-inch (2.5 cm) border around the edges. Add bananas and fold both edges over filling. Place in prepared skillet over medium heat and brown in batches for 3 to 4 minutes or until tortilla is golden brown. Serve immediately.

Variations

Substitute almond butter for the peanut butter and add dates, pecans or almonds for added texture.

These are also great on whole wheat sandwich round thins found in grocery stores.

Grilled Veggie and Goat Cheese Wraps

Fresh veggies, nuts and hummus tucked inside a flavored tortilla are perfect for a healthy weekend or weekday lunch.

Tips

Flavored wraps are widely available, including plain, wheat, pesto, spinach, tomato basil, multigrain and low-carb. Feel free to substitute any of your favorites in these recipes.

Pepitas, or pumpkin seeds, are wonderful roasted or toasted. *To toast pumpkin seeds:* Place seeds on a lightly greased baking sheet in a 300°F (150°C) oven, tossing occasionally, for 45 minutes or until golden brown. You can find them at grocery stores or health food stores. They are a great source of protein, iron and zinc.

4	8-inch (20 cm) spinach-flavored flour tortillas, warmed (see Tips, left)	4
½ cup	Hummus (page 185) or store-bought	125 mL
1 cup	baby spinach leaves	250 mL
1 cup	cucumber slices	250 mL
2	tomatoes, thinly sliced	2
1	red bell pepper, cut into thin slices	1
1 cup	alfalfa sprouts	250 mL
½ cup	whole almonds, toasted	125 mL
½ cup	green pumpkin seeds (pepitas), toasted (see Tips, left)	125 mL
4 oz	crumbled goat cheese	125 g
2 tbsp	butter, softened	30 mL

1. Place tortillas on a work surface. Spread 2 tbsp (30 mL) of the hummus down center of each tortilla. Arrange spinach, cucumber, tomatoes, bell pepper and sprouts over hummus. Top with almonds, pepitas and goat cheese. Fold tortilla in half.

2. In a skillet, heat butter over medium heat. Cook wraps for 3 minutes or until lightly browned and cheese is melted. Serve immediately.

Grilled Vegetable Enchiladas

The zucchini, squash and corn pair wonderfully together in these enchiladas. This is a great vegetarian recipe.

Tip

I used canned corn, but fresh grilled or roasted corn would be great, too.

● **Preheat oven to 350°F (180°C)**

8	6-inch (15 cm) corn tortillas	8
1 cup	thinly sliced zucchini	250 mL
1 cup	thinly sliced yellow summer squash (zucchini)	250 mL
1½ cups	shredded Monterey Jack cheese, divided	375 mL
1 cup	cooked corn kernels, drained (see Tip, left)	250 mL
1 cup	cooked brown rice	250 mL
⅓ cup	sour cream	75 mL
¼ cup	chopped green onions	60 mL
¼ tsp	salt	1 mL
¼ tsp	freshly ground pepper	1 mL
2	cans (each 10 oz/284 mL) diced tomatoes with green chiles	2
8 tsp	olive oil, divided	40 mL

1. Wrap tortillas in foil and bake in preheated oven for 7 minutes. Keep warm.

2. In a pot of boiling water, blanch zucchini and summer squash for 2 minutes. Drain. Combine zucchini, squash, ½ cup (125 mL) of the cheese, corn, rice, sour cream, green onions, salt and pepper.

3. Place tortillas on a work surface. Spoon zucchini mixture equally down center of tortillas and add remaining cheese. Fold both edges over. Heat 1 tsp (5 mL) of the olive oil per tortilla in a large skillet over medium heat. Add tortillas in batches, seam side down, and cook, turning once, for 3 to 4 minutes or until thoroughly heated. Serve immediately.

Easy Meatless Quesadillas

This makes a wonderful vegetarian main dish that even your kids will love.

• **Large nonstick skillet, sprayed with cooking spray**

1 cup	fat-free refried beans	250 mL
1 cup	canned or cooked black beans, drained and rinsed	250 mL
1 cup	salsa	250 mL
4	8-inch (20 cm) whole wheat flour tortillas	4
1 cup	fresh baby spinach leaves	250 mL
1 cup	shredded Monterey Jack cheese	250 mL
1 cup	sliced or chopped tomato	250 mL

Toppings, optional

¼ cup	sliced avocado	60 mL
	Nonfat Greek yogurt	
	Chopped green onions	

1. In a medium bowl, combine refried beans, black beans and salsa.

2. Spread ¼ cup (60 mL) of bean mixture over each tortilla. Top with spinach, cheese and tomato. Fold tortilla in half.

3. Place quesadillas in prepared skillet over medium heat and brown tortillas in batches, for 3 minutes per side or until lightly browned and cheese is melted. Cut each tortilla into 4 wedges and serve with desired toppings. Serve immediately.

Variation

Easy Shrimp Quesadillas: Add 12 oz (375 g) peeled, cooked and deveined large shrimp in Step 2 with spinach, cheese and tomato.

Broccoli Cheese Pitas

Ricotta cheese, feta and walnuts add great flavor and texture to this healthy broccoli-filled grilled cheese.

Tip

To save time, I like to use bagged frozen broccoli florets. Simply thaw them in the microwave per the instructions on the bag and then proceed with the recipe, slightly reducing the cooking time of the broccoli.

1 tbsp	olive oil	15 mL
1 cup	chopped onion	250 mL
4	cloves garlic, minced	4
3 cups	chopped broccoli	750 mL
2 tsp	dried oregano	10 mL
1/2 tsp	hot pepper flakes	2 mL
1/2 tsp	kosher salt	2 mL
1 cup	part-skim ricotta cheese	250 mL
1/2 cup	crumbled reduced-fat feta cheese	125 mL
1/4 cup	chopped walnuts	60 mL
1 tsp	hot pepper sauce, optional	5 mL
4	6- to 8-inch (15 to 20 cm) whole wheat pitas with pockets, halved	4

1. In a nonstick skillet, heat oil over medium heat. Add onion and cook, stirring, for 3 to 4 minutes or until soft. Add garlic, broccoli, oregano, hot pepper flakes and salt. Cook for 5 to 7 minutes or until broccoli is bright green and tender when pierced with a fork.

2. Remove from heat and stir in ricotta, feta and walnuts. Season with hot sauce, if desired. Place pitas on a work surface. Stuff each pocket equally with broccoli mixture.

3. Add more oil to skillet if needed and brown pita halves for 2 to 3 minutes on each side or until toasted and cheese is slightly melted. Serve immediately.

Date, Pecan and Goat Cheese Sandwich

Serves 4

This is one of my all-time favorite recipes in the book. It might sound strange at first, but I promise it is a wonderful fall combination.

- **Preheat heat oven to 350°F (180°C)**
- **Baking sheet, lightly sprayed with cooking spray**

4	6- to 8-inch (15 to 20 cm) flax and oat pitas with pockets	4
¼ cup	peach preserves or jam	60 mL
2 cups	chopped pecans	500 mL
4 tsp	packed brown sugar	20 mL
½ tsp	dried chipotle seasoning	2 mL
1 tbsp	canola oil	15 mL
1 cup	fresh baby arugula leaves	250 mL
1⅓ cups	chopped pitted dates	325 mL
¼ cup	crumbled goat cheese	60 mL

1. Place pita bread on a work surface. Spread equally with preserves. Set aside.

2. In a medium bowl, combine pecans, brown sugar, chipotle and oil. Place on prepared baking sheet. Bake in preheated oven for 5 minutes or until pecans are toasted.

3. Sprinkle arugula equally over preserves. Top with nut mixture, dates and goat cheese. Preheat broiler and broil for 2 to 3 minutes or until cheese is melted. Serve immediately.

Variations

If you can't find peach preserves, you can substitute apricot.

Feel free to use any of your favorite nuts.

Tabbouleh Quinoa Feta Melts

Serves 4

Tabbouleh is an Arab salad traditionally made of cucumber, finely chopped fresh parsley, mint and usually bulgur wheat, onion and garlic. I'm so thankful that my kids love it because it's so good for them.

Tip

If you have any leftover tabbouleh quinoa, it's wonderful served on top of a salad or as a side dish.

● **Preheat broiler with rack 4 inches (10 cm) from heat**

½ cup	quinoa, rinsed and drained	125 mL
¾ cup	chopped tomato (about 1 large)	175 mL
¾ cup	chopped cucumber	175 mL
1 tbsp	chopped green onion	15 mL
1 tbsp	chopped fresh Italian flat-leaf parsley	15 mL
1 tbsp	chopped fresh mint	15 mL
¼ cup	freshly squeezed lemon juice	60 mL
2 tbsp	red wine vinegar	30 mL
2 tbsp	olive oil	30 mL
¼ tsp	freshly ground black pepper	1 mL
4	whole wheat English muffins, split	4
½ cup	arugula leaves	125 mL
¼ cup	crumbled reduced-fat feta cheese	60 mL

1. In a large saucepan over high heat, bring 1 cup (250 mL) water and quinoa to a boil. Reduce heat and simmer for 15 minutes. Drain well and let cool completely.

2. In a large bowl, combine tomato, cucumber, green onion, parsley and mint. Add quinoa and drizzle with lemon juice, vinegar and olive oil. Sprinkle with pepper.

3. Place English muffins on a work surface. Top equally with arugula. Spread quinoa mixture equally on top of muffins over arugula. Sprinkle with feta and broil for 2 minutes or until cheese is melted. Serve immediately.

Variation

Chicken Quinoa Melts: Add 1 cup (250 mL) chopped, cooked chicken to the quinoa mixture.

Grilled Salmon Burgers

Serves 4

This is one of the most popular recipes on my blog www. ingredientsinc.net. I thought I would twist it a bit to create a grilled cheese version.

Tip

Look for canned salmon in the grocery store where canned tuna is sold. I prefer the wild Alaskan sockeye salmon.

- **Panini grill or large skillet, coated with cooking spray**
- **Preheat panini grill to medium, if using**

1/3 cup	plain nonfat Greek yogurt	75 mL
2 tbsp	whole-grain Dijon mustard	30 mL
2	large egg whites	2
1/2 cup	chopped onion	125 mL
1/2 cup	chopped celery	125 mL
1 cup	panko bread crumbs, divided	250 mL
1/4 tsp	chopped fresh chives	1 mL
1/4 tsp	chopped fresh basil	1 mL
1/8 tsp	freshly ground black pepper	0.5 mL
2	cans (each 7 oz/213 g) wild Alaskan red salmon, skin removed and drained (see Tip, left)	2
4 tsp	olive oil	20 mL
4	whole wheat hamburger buns, toasted and split	4
4	slices part-skim mozzarella cheese	4
	Fresh basil sprigs, optional	

1. In a large bowl, combine yogurt, mustard and egg whites. Set aside.

2. In a nonstick skillet coated with cooking spray, sauté onion and celery over medium-high heat for 4 minutes or until tender. Let cool slightly.

3. In a large bowl, combine onion mixture, 1/2 cup (125 mL) of the bread crumbs, chives, basil and pepper. Add salmon and toss gently. Cover and refrigerate and let chill for 10 minutes.

4. Divide salmon mixture into 4 equal patties, about $1/2$ inch (1 cm) thick. Coat patties equally with remaining $1/2$ cup (125 mL) bread crumbs.

5. In a large nonstick skillet, heat oil over medium-high heat. Fry patties, turning once, for 4 minutes per side or until lightly browned and hot in the center.

6. Place hamburger buns on a work surface. Arrange salmon burgers on buns and top with cheese. Garnish with basil sprigs, if using. Top with remaining buns. Return to skillet over medium heat or place in preheated panini grill coated with cooking spray and cook, turning once, for 3 more minutes per side or until cheese melts and buns are slightly toasted. Serve immediately.

Variation

Grilled Tuna Burgers: Substitute canned tuna for the salmon in this recipe.

Meatless

Classic Grilled Two Cheese

This is back to the basics and a classic. I love to serve it with a creamy tomato soup in the wintertime.

- **Panini grill or large skillet**
- **Preheat panini grill to medium, if using**

8	slices white or whole-grain bread (½-inch/1 cm thick slices)	8
2 tbsp	butter or margarine, softened	30 mL
4 oz	Muenster cheese, thinly sliced	125 g
4 oz	Cheddar cheese, thinly sliced	125 g

1. Brush one side of each bread slice with butter. Place on a work surface, buttered side down. Top 4 bread slices equally with Muenster and Cheddar cheeses. Cover with remaining bread slices, buttered side up, and press gently.

2. Place sandwiches on preheated panini grill or in a large skillet over medium heat and cook, turning once if using a skillet, for 3 to 4 minutes or until golden brown and cheese is melted. Serve immediately.

Grilled Guacomento

Serves 4

This idea of blending guacamole and pimiento cheese came from my friend, Kiel, and when she told me about it, I was so excited to make it. When I made these, everyone asked, "Why didn't I think of that?"

- **Panini grill or large skillet**
- **Preheat panini grill to medium, if using**

8	slices whole wheat bread (½-inch/1 cm thick slices)	8
¼ cup	butter or margarine, softened	60 mL
½ cup	Guacamole (page 180) or store-bought	125 mL
1 cup	fresh spinach leaves	250 mL
2	tomatoes, thinly sliced	2
½ cup	Pimiento Cheese (page 193) or store-bought	125 mL

1. Brush one side of each bread slice with butter. Place on a work surface, buttered side down. Spread guacamole equally on bread slices. Top 4 bread slices equally with spinach, tomatoes and pimiento cheese. Cover with remaining bread slices, buttered side up, and press together gently.

2. Place sandwiches on preheated panini grill or in a large skillet over medium heat and cook, turning once if using a skillet, for 3 to 4 minutes or until golden brown and cheese is melted. Serve immediately.

California Grilled Cheese

I love making California-style sandwiches. They are always fabulous and seem so fresh and healthy.

- Panini grill or large skillet
- Preheat panini grill to medium, if using

8	slices whole-grain bread ($\frac{1}{2}$-inch/1 cm thick slices)	8
2 tbsp	olive oil	30 mL
4	slices Havarti cheese	4
2	avocados, sliced	2
2	tomatoes, thinly sliced	2
1 cup	alfalfa sprouts	250 mL

1. Brush one side of each bread slice with olive oil. Place on a work surface, oiled side down. Top 4 bread slices equally with cheese, avocados, tomatoes and sprouts. Cover with remaining bread slices, oiled side up, and press gently.

2. Place sandwiches on preheated panini grill or in a large skillet over medium heat and cook, turning once if using a skillet, for 3 to 4 minutes or until golden brown and cheese is melted. Serve immediately.

Variation

Substitute provolone or Muenster cheese for the Havarti.

On-the-Grill Grilled Cheese

Serves 4

For something different, I like to make my grilled cheese on the grill outside. My kids think it's so different, and it's really just as simple.

Tip

Make sure the grill is lightly greased so the sandwiches don't stick.

● **Preheat lightly greased barbecue grill to medium**

8	slices whole-grain bread (½-inch/1 cm thick slices)	8
¼ cup	butter or margarine, softened	60 mL
4	slices Colby cheese	4
4	slices Havarti cheese	4
2	tomatoes, thinly sliced	2

1. Brush one side of each bread slice with butter. Place on a work surface, buttered side down. Top 4 bread slices equally with Colby and Havarti cheeses and tomato slices. Cover with remaining bread slices, buttered side up, and press gently.

2. Place on prepared grill rack and grill, turning once, for 3 to 4 minutes or until golden brown and cheese is melted. Serve immediately.

Southwestern Grilled Cheese

I love this grilled cheese recipe. I can never go wrong with Southwestern foods. Serve with an avocado salad for a complete meal.

Tip

Jalapeños can be found in the produce section at almost any grocery store. Store them in a plastic bag in the refrigerator for up to 1 week.

- **Panini grill or large skillet**
- **Preheat panini grill to medium, if using**

8	slices white or whole-grain bread (½-inch/1 cm thick slices)	8
2 tbsp	butter or margarine, softened	30 mL
4	slices pepper Jack cheese	4
2	tomatoes, thinly sliced	2
2	avocados, thinly sliced	2

Toppings, optional

Salsa

Sour cream

Chopped jalapeños

Freshly chopped cilantro

1. Brush one side of each bread slice with butter. Place on a work surface, buttered side down. Top 4 bread slices equally with cheese, tomato slices and avocado slices. Cover with remaining bread slices, buttered side up, and press together gently.

2. Place sandwiches on preheated panini grill or in a large skillet over medium heat and cook, turning once if using a skillet, for 3 to 4 minutes or until golden brown and cheese is melted. Serve immediately with desired toppings.

Variation

Substitute nonfat Greek yogurt for the sour cream. It tastes great, has zero fat and has a lot of protein.

Provençal Panini

Serves 4

I love to serve this sandwich with a Caesar salad for a simple meal.

Tip

If you want to limit fat intake, use dehydrated sun-dried tomatoes. They even sell them already sliced.

- **Panini grill or large skillet**
- **Preheat panini grill to medium, if using**

8	slices white or whole-grain bread (½-inch/1 cm thick slices)	8
2 tbsp	olive oil	30 mL
2	tomatoes, thinly sliced	2
1 cup	sun-dried tomatoes, packed in oil, drained	250 mL
¾ cup	sliced kalamata olives	175 mL
4	slices mozzarella cheese	4
½ cup	freshly grated Parmesan cheese	125 mL
½ tsp	hot pepper flakes	2 mL

1. Brush one side of each bread slice with olive oil. Place on a work surface, oiled side down. Top 4 bread slices equally with tomatoes, sun-dried tomatoes, olives and mozzarella and Parmesan cheeses. Sprinkle equally with hot pepper flakes. Cover with remaining bread slices, oiled side up, and press together gently.

2. Place sandwiches on preheated panini grill or in a large skillet over medium heat and cook, turning once if using a skillet, for 3 to 4 minutes or until golden brown and cheese is melted. Serve immediately.

Seasonal Vegetable Panini

Serves 4

These are one of my favorite panini sandwiches. I love to serve them with minestrone soup for a soup and sandwich night.

Tip

Since eggplant can often taste bitter depending on the variety, I like to sprinkle it with salt and let stand for about 30 minutes. Then rinse off and cook.

- **Large baking sheet, lined with parchment paper**
- **Preheat oven to 400°F (200°C)**
- **Panini grill or large skillet**
- **Preheat panini grill to medium, if using**

1	medium eggplant, peeled and sliced into $1/4$-inch (0.5 cm) slices (see Tip, left)	1
7 tbsp	olive oil, divided	105 mL
$1/2$ tsp	sea salt, divided	2 mL
$1/2$ tsp	freshly ground black pepper, divided	2 mL
6	Roma (plum) tomatoes, thinly sliced	6
2	cloves garlic, minced	2
8	slices ciabatta bread or Italian bread ($1/2$-inch/1 cm thick slices)	8
4 oz	crumbled goat cheese	125 g
4	slices mozzarella cheese	4
$1/2$ cup	chopped fresh basil	125 mL

1. On prepared baking sheet, place eggplant in a single layer. Drizzle with 3 tbsp (45 mL) of the olive oil. Sprinkle with $1/4$ tsp (1 mL) of the salt and $1/4$ tsp (1 mL) of the pepper. Bake in preheated oven for 20 minutes or until eggplant is tender.

2. Place tomatoes on prepared baking sheet and drizzle with 2 tbsp (30 mL) of olive oil, garlic and remaining salt and pepper. Bake in preheated oven for 15 minutes. Set aside.

3. Brush one side of each bread slice with remaining 2 tbsp (30 mL) of oil. Place on work surface, oiled side down. Spread goat cheese on one side of each bread slice. Top 4 slices equally with mozzarella, eggplant, tomatoes and basil. Cover with remaining bread, oiled side up, and press together gently.

4. Place sandwiches on preheated panini grill or in a large skillet over medium heat and cook, turning once if using a skillet, for 5 minutes or until golden brown and cheese is melted. Serve immediately.

Grilled Swiss, Artichokes and Olives

This makes great use of artichokes and is a delicious vegetarian grilled cheese. It's perfect for lunch or a weeknight dinner served with a tossed salad.

- **Panini grill or large skillet**
- **Preheat panini grill to medium, if using**

8	slices multigrain, country whole wheat or oat bread (½-inch/1 cm thick slices)	8
2 tbsp	butter or margarine, softened	30 mL
2 tbsp	coarse-grain mustard	30 mL
1 cup	drained canned chopped artichokes	250 mL
¾ cup	baby spinach leaves	175 mL
4	Swiss cheese slices	4
1 cup	thinly sliced black olives	250 mL

1. Brush one side of each bread slice with butter. Place on a work surface, buttered side down. Spread mustard equally over 4 slices. Top equally with artichokes, spinach, cheese and olives. Cover with remaining bread slices, buttered side up, and press together gently.

2. Place sandwiches on preheated panini grill or in a large skillet over medium heat and cook, turning once if using a skillet, for 3 to 4 minutes or until golden brown and cheese is melted. Serve immediately.

Smoked Mozzarella, Arugula and Tomato

Serves 4

Using peppery arugula and smoked mozzarella makes this grilled cheese unique. I love to serve this sandwich when I am entertaining.

Tips

Make sure you wash arugula well before using because dirt clings to the leaves easily.

Do not store tomatoes in the refrigerator as cool temperatures reduce their flavor. Store at room temperature. Once ripened, use within a few days.

- **Panini grill or large skillet**
- **Preheat panini grill to medium, if using**

8	slices Italian bread ($\frac{1}{2}$-inch/1 cm thick slices)	8
2 tbsp	butter or margarine, softened	30 mL
$\frac{1}{4}$ cup	Basil Pesto (page 181) or store-bought	60 mL
4 oz	smoked mozzarella, thinly sliced	125 g
1 cup	arugula leaves (see Tips, left)	250 mL
2	tomatoes, thinly sliced (see Tips, left)	2

1. Brush one side of each bread slice with butter. Place on a work surface, buttered side down. Spread 4 bread slices equally with pesto. Top equally with cheese, arugula and tomatoes. Cover with remaining bread slices, buttered side up, and press together gently.

2. Place sandwiches on preheated panini grill or in a large skillet over medium heat and cook, turning once if using a skillet, for 3 to 4 minutes or until golden brown and cheese is melted. Serve immediately.

Variation

Watercress also works great in this recipe instead of the arugula.

Lasagna Grilled Cheese

Serves 4

When I don't have time to make lasagna, I cook these up really quickly. The kids love them!

Tip

If you're short on time, purchase already shredded cheese. If you do have time, grate your own for better quality.

- Panini grill or large skillet
- Preheat panini grill to medium, if using

8	slices Italian bread (1/2-inch/1 cm thick slices)	8
1/4 cup	butter or margarine, softened	60 mL
1/4 cup	marinara sauce	60 mL
8	thin slices mozzarella cheese	8
1 cup	freshly grated Parmesan cheese (see Tip, left)	250 mL

1. Brush one side of each bread slice with butter. Place on a work surface, buttered side down. Spread 4 bread slices equally with marinara sauce. Top equally with mozzarella and Parmesan. Cover with remaining bread slices, buttered side up, and press together gently.

2. Place sandwiches on preheated panini grill or in a large skillet over medium heat and cook, turning once if using a skillet, for 3 to 4 minutes or until golden brown and cheese is melted. Serve immediately.

Variation

Add 1 1/2 cups (375 mL) baby spinach leaves with the cheeses in Step 1 and proceed as directed.

Feta, Tomato and Basil Grilled Cheese

Serves 4

This sandwich is filled with the most popular ingredients at my house. This is so easy and a crowd (and family) pleaser.

Tip

To slice basil more quickly, roll up a small bunch of leaves and cut into shreds with a knife or kitchen shears. This is called chiffonade.

- **Panini grill or large skillet**
- **Preheat panini grill to medium, if using**

8	slices Italian bread (½-inch/1 cm thick slices)	8
½ cup	olive oil	125 mL
12	large fresh tomatoes, thinly sliced	12
½ cup	chopped fresh basil (see Tip, left)	125 mL
4	slices provolone cheese	4
½ cup	crumbled feta cheese	125 mL

1. Brush one side of each bread slice with olive oil. Place on a work surface, oiled side down. Top 4 bread slices equally with tomatoes, basil, provolone and feta. Cover with remaining bread slices, oiled side up, and press together gently.

2. Place sandwiches on preheated panini grill or in a large skillet over medium-high heat and cook, turning once if using a skillet, for 3 to 4 minutes or until golden brown and cheese is melted. Serve immediately.

Grilled Roasted Pepper and Feta

Serves 4 to 6

I believe roasted red peppers are great with any cheese, but I am very fond of this version with feta.

Tip

You can also roast bell peppers in the microwave. *To roast peppers in microwave:* Place peppers in a microwave-safe dish and cover with an airtight lid to allow for the steam to build up inside. Microwave on High for 3 to 4 minutes. Turn peppers with tongs, cover and microwave for 6 minutes more or until peppers look blistered. Cover and let stand for 10 to 20 minutes or until cool.

- **Preheat broiler**
- **Panini grill or large skillet**
- **Preheat panini grill to medium, if using**

4	large red or yellow bell peppers (see Tip, left)	4
3 tbsp	olive oil, divided	45 mL
1 tbsp	balsamic vinegar	15 mL
2	cloves garlic, minced	2
1/2 tsp	sea salt	2 mL
1/2 tsp	freshly ground black pepper	2 mL
1	large ciabatta or French bread, cut into 1/2-inch/1 cm thick slices	1
1 cup	fresh baby spinach leaves	250 mL
1/2 cup	fresh basil leaves	125 mL
1 cup	crumbled feta cheese	250 mL

1. Place peppers on a large baking sheet. Broil for 7 to 12 minutes or until entire pepper skin has turned black and blistery. Immediately place peppers in an airtight container such as a bowl with a lid or plastic bag and seal for 15 to 20 minutes. Peel off the blackened skin. Cut peppers in half, core and remove seeds. Slice peppers into strips and place in a bowl.

2. In a small bowl, combine 1 tbsp (15 mL) of the olive oil, vinegar, garlic, salt and pepper. Pour over peppers. Cover and refrigerate for at least 1 hour.

3. To assemble, brush one side of each bread slice with remaining 2 tbsp (30 mL) olive oil. Place on a work surface, oiled side down. Top 4 bread slices equally with spinach, basil, roasted pepper mixture and feta. Cover with remaining bread slices, oiled side up, and press together gently.

4. Place sandwiches on preheated panini grill or in a large skillet over medium heat and cook, turning once if using a skillet, for 3 to 4 minutes or until golden brown and cheese is melted. Serve immediately.

Eggplant and Pesto Grilled Cheese

Serves 4

Serve this sandwich with a glass of Chianti and a tossed salad for a winning sandwich night meal.

Tip

If you decide to use fresh sliced mozzarella instead of regular mozzarella, it adds a creamier texture.

- **Preheat greased barbecue grill to medium**
- **Panini grill or large skillet**
- **Preheat panini grill to medium, if using**

1	medium eggplant, sliced into 1/4-inch (0.5 cm) slices	1
1/4 cup + 2 tbsp	olive oil, divided	90 mL
2 tbsp	balsamic vinegar	30 mL
1/8 tsp	salt	0.5 mL
1/8 tsp	freshly ground black pepper	0.5 mL
2	large tomatoes, sliced	2
8	slices Italian or sourdough bread (1/2-inch/1 cm thick slices)	8
1/2 cup	Basil Pesto (page 181) or store-bought	125 mL
4	slices mozzarella cheese	4

1. Coat eggplant with 1/4 cup (60 mL) of the olive oil and vinegar. Season with salt and pepper. Grill on preheated grill for 5 minutes or until tender. Add tomatoes and grill for 1 minute per side.

2. Brush one side of each bread slice with remaining 2 tbsp (30 mL) olive oil. Place on a work surface, oiled side down. Spread all slices equally with pesto. Top 4 slices with eggplant, tomatoes and cheese. Cover with remaining bread slices, oiled side up, and press together gently.

3. Place sandwiches on preheated grill, panini or in a skillet over medium heat and cook, turning once if using a skillet, for 3 to 4 minutes or until golden brown and cheese is melted. Serve immediately.

Grilled Zucchini with Cilantro Pesto

I love the fresh cilantro paired with the zucchini and squash in this vegetarian delight. Cooking the zucchini and cilantro like this also makes a great side dish to serve with pork, chicken or seafood.

Tips

Store pesto in an airtight container in the refrigerator for up to 1 week or freeze for up to 6 months.

You could also use store-bought pesto here. Just add 2 tbsp (30 mL) cilantro and process in a food processor until smooth.

- Panini grill or large skillet
- Preheat panini grill to medium, if using

2 tbsp	olive oil	30 mL
2	medium zucchini, unpeeled and cut into 1/4-inch (0.5 cm) round slices	2
1	medium yellow summer squash (zucchini), unpeeled and cut into 1/2-inch (1 cm) round slices	1
1/2	small onion, thinly sliced	1/2
1/4 tsp	salt	1 mL
1/4 tsp	freshly ground black pepper	1 mL
2 tbsp	freshly squeezed lemon juice	30 mL
8	slices whole wheat bread (1/2-inch/1 cm thick slices)	8
1/4 cup	butter or margarine, softened	60 mL
1/4 cup	Cilantro Pesto (page 184) (see Tips, left)	60 mL
4	slices Monterey Jack or pepper Jack cheese	4

1. In a large skillet, heat oil over medium heat. Add zucchini, squash and onion and cook, stirring frequently, for 5 to 7 minutes or until tender. Sprinkle with salt and pepper. Drizzle with lemon juice.

2. Brush one side of each bread slice with butter. Place on a work surface, buttered side down. Spread 4 bread slices equally with Cilantro Pesto. Top equally with vegetables and cheese. Cover with remaining bread slices, buttered side up, and press together gently.

3. Place sandwiches on preheated panini grill or in a large skillet over medium heat and cook, turning once if using a skillet, for 3 to 4 minutes or until golden brown and cheese is melted. Serve immediately.

Grilled Asparagus, Swiss and Pesto

This sandwich is a winner. Try it, and you will see. I also like to use flour tortillas and make this as a wrap sandwich.

Tip

This would be great served with fontina instead of or in addition to Swiss.

- **Preheat oven to 350°F (180°C)**
- **Panini grill or large skillet**
- **Preheat panini grill to medium, if using**

1 lb	asparagus, cut into 2-inch (5 cm) pieces	500 g
¼ tsp	salt	1 mL
¼ tsp	freshly ground black pepper	1 mL
2 tbsp	olive oil	30 mL
8	slices sourdough bread (½-inch/1 cm thick slices)	8
2 tbsp	butter or margarine, softened	30 mL
½ cup	Basil Pesto (page 181) or store-bought	125 mL
4	slices Swiss cheese	4

1. Season asparagus with salt and pepper and drizzle with olive oil. Place on a large baking sheet and bake in preheated oven for 10 minutes or until tender. Let cool.

2. Brush one side of each bread slice with butter. Place on a work surface, buttered side down. Spread bread slices equally with pesto. Top 4 slices equally with asparagus and cheese. Cover with remaining slices, buttered side up, and press together gently.

3. Place sandwiches on preheated panini grill or in a large skillet over medium heat and cook, turning once if using a skillet, for 3 to 4 minutes or until golden brown and cheese is melted. Serve immediately.

Variation

Add turkey or grilled chicken for added protein.

Grilled Sun-Dried Tomato Pesto and Vegetables

If you like sun-dried tomatoes as much as I do, you will love this vegetarian combination.

Tip

I like to use the dry-packed sun-dried tomatoes because they are lower in fat, and this sandwich already has big tomato flavor from the pesto. You can usually find them where the other sun-dried tomatoes are sold in the grocery store.

- **Panini grill or large skillet**
- **Preheat panini grill to medium, if using**

8	slices whole wheat bread (½-inch/1 cm thick slices)	8
2 tbsp	butter or margarine, softened	30 mL
¼ cup	Sun-Dried Tomato Pesto (page 182)	60 mL
1 cup	thinly sliced cucumber	250 mL
1 cup	thinly sliced tomatoes	250 mL
1 cup	dry-packed sun-dried tomatoes (see Tip, left)	250 mL
4 oz	Asiago cheese, thinly sliced	125 g

1. Brush one side of each bread slice with butter. Place on a work surface, buttered side down. Spread 4 bread slices equally with pesto. Top with cucumber, tomatoes, sun-dried tomatoes and cheese. Cover with remaining bread slices, buttered side up, and press together gently.

2. Place sandwiches on preheated panini grill or in a large skillet over medium heat and cook, turning once if using a skillet, for 3 to 4 minutes or until golden brown and cheese is melted. Serve immediately.

Variations

Use Italian or sourdough bread instead of whole wheat.

This also works great by substituting Basil Pesto (page 181) for the Sun-Dried Tomato Pesto.

Beef

Grilled Roast Beef and Sweet Red Pepper Relish

Serves 4

Sweet Red Pepper Relish is the star ingredient in this gooey grilled cheese bursting with flavors.

Tip

To store fresh basil: Wrap stems in moist paper towels and refrigerate in a tightly sealed plastic bag for up to 2 days. For best flavor, use the basil as soon as you can.

- Panini grill or large skillet
- Preheat panini grill to medium, if using

8	slices sourdough bread (½-inch/1 cm thick slices)	8
¼ cup	butter or margarine, softened	60 mL
¼ cup	Homemade Mayonnaise (page 188) or store-bought	60 mL
12 oz	thinly sliced roast beef	375 g
½ cup	shredded mozzarella cheese	125 mL
1 cup	fresh basil leaves (see Tip, left)	250 mL
1½ cups	Sweet Pepper Relish (page 177) or store-bought relish	375 mL

1. Brush one side of each bread slice with butter. Place on a work surface, buttered side down. Spread 4 bread slices equally with mayonnaise. Top equally with roast beef, cheese, basil and Sweet Pepper Relish. Cover with remaining bread slices, buttered side up, and press together gently.

2. Place sandwiches on preheated panini grill or in a large skillet over medium heat and cook, turning once if using a skillet, for 3 to 4 minutes or until golden brown and cheese is melted. Serve immediately.

Grilled Roast Beef and Stilton

Stilton is a semisoft, crumbly cheese that is similar to blue cheese. It is terrific paired with roast beef and peppery arugula.

- **Panini grill or large skillet**
- **Preheat panini grill to medium, if using**

8	slices whole wheat bread	8
¼ cup	butter or margarine, softened	60 mL
¼ cup	Homemade Mayonnaise or Fresh Basil Aïoli (pages 188 and 189) or store-bought	60 mL
12 oz	thinly sliced roast beef	375 g
1 cup	arugula leaves	250 mL
2	tomatoes, thinly sliced	2
1 cup	crumbled Stilton cheese or your favorite blue cheese	250 mL

1. Brush one side of each bread slice with butter. Place on a work surface, buttered side down. Spread 4 bread slices equally with mayonnaise. Top equally with roast beef, arugula, tomatoes and cheese. Cover with remaining bread slices, buttered side up, and press together gently.

2. Place sandwiches on preheated panini grill or in a large skillet over medium heat and cook, turning once if using a skillet, for 3 to 4 minutes or until golden brown and cheese is melted. Serve immediately.

Grilled Roast Beef and Manchego

Take deli roast beef to the next level with the flavors and textures of this fabulous Spanish-style cheese.

Tip

Dijon mustard originated in France and is made from brown mustard seeds and white wine, thus is more flavorful than yellow mustard.

- **Panini grill or large skillet**
- **Preheat panini grill to medium, if using**

8	slices sourdough bread (½-inch/1 cm thick slices)	8
2 tbsp	butter or margarine, softened	30 mL
½ cup	Dijon mustard (see Tip, left)	125 mL
8 oz	thinly sliced roasted beef	250 g
4 oz	Manchego cheese, thinly sliced	125 g
1 cup	watercress leaves	250 mL
¾ cup	Spanish olives, sliced	175 mL

1. Brush one side of each bread slice with butter. Place on a work surface, buttered side down. Spread tops of each bread slice equally with Dijon mustard. Top 4 bread slices equally with roast beef, cheese, watercress and olives. Cover with remaining bread slices, buttered side up, and press together gently. Press bread slices together gently, buttered side up.

2. Place sandwiches on preheated panini grill or in a large skillet over medium heat and cook, turning once if using a skillet, for 3 to 4 minutes or until golden brown and cheese is melted. Serve immediately.

Variations

If you're having trouble finding watercress, use green leafy lettuce or baby spinach.

Substitute 8 oz (250 g) thinly sliced prosciutto or turkey for the roast beef.

Grilled Roast Beef, Nectarine and Brie

Serves 4

Since I love all of these ingredients, I thought they would pair together beautifully. This is a favorite when I have fresh nectarines.

- **Panini grill or large skillet**
- **Preheat panini grill to medium, if using**

8	slices multigrain bread (1/2-inch/1 cm thick slices)	8
2 tbsp	butter or margarine, softened	30 mL
1/4 cup	liquid honey	60 mL
12 oz	thinly sliced roast beef	375 g
2	nectarines, thinly sliced	2
4 oz	Brie, thinly sliced	125 g

1. Brush one side of each bread slice with butter. Place on a work surface, buttered side down. Spread 4 bread slices equally with honey. Top with roast beef, nectarine slices and Brie. Cover with remaining 4 bread slices, buttered side up, and press together gently.

2. Place sandwiches on preheated panini grill or in a large skillet over medium heat and cook, turning once if using a skillet, for 3 to 4 minutes or until golden brown and cheese is melted. Serve immediately.

Roast Beef and Fontina Focaccia Panini

Serves 4			

Serve this sandwich with a spinach salad and fresh fruit for a complete meal.

- Panini grill or large skillet
- Preheat panini grill to medium, if using

4	4-inch (10 cm) focaccia, halved horizontally	4
¼ cup	olive oil, divided	60 mL
¼ cup	Basil Pesto (page 181) or store-bought	60 mL
4 oz	sliced turkey	125 g
2 oz	sliced roast beef	60 g
2 cups	arugula	500 mL
1	tomato, thinly sliced	1
4 oz	thinly sliced fontina	125 g
2 tbsp	balsamic vinegar	30 mL
⅛ tsp	freshly ground black pepper	0.5 mL

1. Place focaccia, cut side down, on a work surface and brush crusts with olive oil. Turn over and spread equally with pesto. Top 4 halves equally with turkey, roast beef, arugula, tomato and cheese. Drizzle with balsamic vinegar and sprinkle with pepper. Top with remaining focaccia, oiled side up, and press together gently.

2. Place sandwiches on a preheated panini grill or in a skillet over medium heat and cook, turning once if using a skillet, for 3 to 4 minutes or until golden brown and cheese is melted. Serve immediately.

Variation

Substitute 8 Italian bread slices or sourdough bread for the focaccia in this recipe.

The Pilgrim

This sandwich became popular in the 1950s, but it still is a hit today, especially during Thanksgiving.

- **Panini grill or large skillet**
- **Preheat panini grill to medium, if using**

8	slices pumpernickel bread (1/2-inch/1 cm thick slices)	8
2 tbsp	butter or margarine, softened	30 mL
1/4 cup	Dijon mustard	60 mL
8 oz	thinly sliced roast beef	250 g
1 cup	baby spinach leaves	250 mL
4 oz	Gouda cheese, thinly sliced	125 g
3/4 cup	dried cranberries	175 mL

1. Brush one side of each bread slice with butter. Place on a work surface, buttered side down. Spread 4 bread slices equally with Dijon mustard. Top equally with roast beef, spinach, cheese and cranberries. Cover with remaining bread slices, buttered side up, and press together gently.

2. Place sandwiches on preheated panini grill or in a large skillet over medium heat and cook, turning once if using a skillet, for 3 to 4 minutes or until golden brown and cheese is melted. Serve immediately.

Grilled Steak, Beets and Parmesan

Serves 4

The sweetness of beets and fresh Parmesan create an upscale grilled cheese. People love when I serve these sandwiches because they are so unique.

Tip

Instead of fresh beets, use 1 cup (250 mL) sliced canned beets.

- **Panini grill or large skillet**
- **Preheat panini grill to medium, if using**

8	slices sourdough bread (½-inch/1 cm thick slices)	8
2 tbsp	olive oil	30 mL
1½ cups	thinly sliced cooked steak	375 g
1 cup	thinly sliced beets (see Tip, left)	250 mL
½ cup	baby spinach leaves	125 mL
½ cup	freshly grated Parmesan cheese	125 mL

1. Brush one side of each bread slice with olive oil. Place on a work surface, oiled side down. Top 4 bread slices with steak, beets, spinach and Parmesan. Cover with remaining bread slices, oiled side up, and press together gently.

2. Place sandwiches on preheated panini grill or in a large skillet over medium heat and cook, turning once if using a skillet, for 3 to 4 minutes or until golden brown and cheese is melted. Serve immediately.

Grilled Steak and Blue Cheese

Serves 4

This sandwich is awesome served with a salad of iceberg lettuce wedges topped with diced tomatoes, red onion and crumbled blue cheese.

Tip

Broil steak 5½ inches (14 cm) from heat. (If using an electric oven, leave door partially open.) Or grill over medium-high heat for 6 to 8 minutes per side for well done. Cut steak across the grain into thin slices.

- **Panini grill or large skillet**
- **Preheat panini grill to medium, if using**

¼ cup	olive oil	60 mL
1 tbsp	chopped fresh parsley	15 mL
1 tbsp	chopped fresh thyme	15 mL
1	clove garlic, minced	1
½ tsp	salt	2 mL
½ tsp	freshly ground black pepper	2 mL
8	slices French bread (½-inch/1 cm slices)	8
2 tbsp	butter or margarine, softened	30 mL
1 lb	grilled steak, very thinly sliced (see Tip, left)	500 g
½ cup	baby spinach leaves	125 mL
½ cup	crumbled blue cheese	125 mL

1. In a small bowl, combine olive oil, parsley, thyme, garlic, salt and pepper.

2. Brush one side of each bread slice with butter. Place on a work surface, buttered side down. Spread 4 bottom halves equally with oil mixture. Top other 4 bread slices equally with steak, spinach and blue cheese. Press slices together gently.

3. Place sandwiches on preheated panini grill or in a large skillet over medium heat and cook, turning once if using a skillet, for 3 to 4 minutes or until golden brown and cheese is melted. Serve immediately.

Pastrami and White Cheddar Grilled Cheese

This grilled cheese is my oldest son's favorite. He suggested it one day, and now it's a keeper.

Tip

If you can't find white Cheddar, feel free to substitute equal amounts of regular Cheddar.

- **Panini grill or large skillet**
- **Preheat panini grill to medium, if using**

8	slices rye bread (1/2-inch/1 cm thick slices)	8
2 tbsp	butter or margarine, softened	30 mL
1/4 cup	spicy deli or Dijon mustard	60 mL
12 oz	sliced pastrami	375 g
4	slices white Cheddar cheese	4

1. Brush one side of each bread slice with butter. Place on a work surface, buttered side down. Spread 4 bread slices equally with mustard. Top equally with pastrami and cheese. Cover with remaining bread slices, buttered side up, and press gently.

2. Place sandwiches on preheated panini grill or in a large skillet over medium heat and cook, turning once if using a skillet, for 3 to 4 minutes or until golden brown and cheese is melted. Serve immediately.

Grilled Carnegie Sandwich

Serves 4

This sandwich is similar to one at the Carnegie Deli in New York. I love serving these with matzo ball or chicken and rice soup.

- **Panini grill or large skillet**
- **Preheat panini grill to medium, if using**

8	slices rye bread (½-inch/1 cm thick slices)	8
2 tbsp	butter or margarine, softened	30 mL
¾ cup	deli mustard	175 mL
8 oz	thinly sliced pastrami	250 g
3	kosher dill pickles, thinly sliced	3
4	slices Swiss cheese	4

1. Brush one side of each bread slice with butter. Place on a work surface, buttered side down. Spread mustard on tops of bread slices. Top 4 bread slices equally with pastrami, pickles and cheese. Cover with remaining bread slices, buttered side up, and press gently.

2. Place sandwiches on preheated panini grill or in a large skillet over medium-high heat and cook, turning once if using a skillet, for 3 to 4 minutes or until golden brown and cheese is melted. Serve immediately.

Variation

Substitute Thousand Island dressing for the deli mustard.

Grilled Cheese Burgers

Serves 4

I know of a few popular restaurants that serve hamburgers between grilled cheese sandwiches. When I made these, my children's eyes got so big.

Tip

Feel free to cook the burger and grilled cheese in a large skillet over medium-high heat for 4 minutes per side or until an instant-read thermometer registers 160°F (71°C).

- **Preheat greased barbecue grill to medium-high heat (see Tip, left)**
- **Instant-read thermometer**

1½ lbs	ground sirloin	750 g
1 tbsp	Worcestershire sauce	15 mL
¼ tsp	salt	1 mL
¼ tsp	freshly ground black pepper	1 mL
8	slices sourdough (½-inch/1 cm thick slices)	8
¼ cup	butter or margarine, softened	60 mL
4	slices Cheddar cheese	4

Toppings, optional

Lettuce

Tomato slices

Pickles

Ketchup

1. In a large bowl, combine beef, Worcestershire, salt and pepper. Form into 4 equal patties, about ¾ inch (2 cm) thick.

2. Brush one side of bread slices with butter. Place on a work surface, buttered side down. Top 4 bread slices equally with cheese. Cover with remaining bread slices, buttered side up, and press together gently.

3. Grill hamburgers for 5 minutes per side or until an instant-read thermometer registers 160°F (71°C). Set aside.

4. Reduce barbecue grill to medium heat. Place sandwiches on preheated grill, buttered side down, over medium heat and cook, turning once, for 2 minutes per side or until golden brown and cheese is melted. Place hamburgers between each grilled cheese sandwich, pressing together gently. Top with desired toppings and serve immediately.

Classic Patty Melts

I never really had patty melts growing up. I had a friend that used to tell me her mom served them with cut-up fresh fruit on the side for a wonderful summertime meal.

Tip

I like to purchase ground sirloin because it's leaner, has less fat than ground beef, and it tastes great!

- Preheat greased barbecue grill to medium-high, if using
- Instant-read thermometer

1½ lbs	ground sirloin	750 g
2 tbsp	Worcestershire sauce	30 mL
¼ tsp	kosher salt	1 mL
¼ tsp	freshly ground black pepper	1 mL
1 tbsp	butter or margarine	15 mL
1 tsp	olive oil	5 mL
8 oz	sliced fresh mushrooms	250 g
½ cup	sliced onion	125 mL
4	slices Swiss cheese	4
8	slices rye bread, toasted	4
2 tbsp	melted butter	30 mL

1. In a large bowl, combine sirloin, Worcestershire sauce, salt and pepper. Shape into 4 equal patties, about ¾ inch (2 cm) thick.

2. In a large skillet, melt butter over medium-high heat. Place burgers on skillet or grill, if using, and fry over medium-high heat for 6 to 8 minutes per side or until an instant-read thermometer registers 160°F (71°C).

3. In another large skillet, heat oil over medium heat. Add mushrooms and onion and cook, stirring frequently, for 5 minutes or until golden. Top each burger with one cheese slice and melt.

4. Place bread slices on a work surface. Brush melted butter over half. Place 4 slices in skillet, buttered side down. Top with burger, mushrooms, onion and top with remaining bread. Fry until bread is lightly browned on each side and cheese is melted. Serve immediately.

Variation

Light Patty Melt: Add 4 slices turkey bacon, use reduced-fat cheese and serve open-faced in lettuce wraps.

Chicken and Turkey

Chicken, Apple and Smoked Gouda

Serves 4

The roasted chicken pairs nicely with the sweetness of the apple and smokiness of the Gouda cheese.

Tip

I use one deli-style rotisserie chicken. It yields the perfect amount.

- **Panini grill or large skillet**
- **Preheat panini grill to medium, if using**

8	slices Italian or multigrain bread (½-inch/1 cm thick slices)	8
¼ cup	butter or margarine, softened	60 mL
¼ cup	Homemade Mayonnaise (page 188) or store-bought	60 mL
2 cups	thinly sliced roasted or grilled chicken (see Tip, left)	500 mL
1 cup	baby spinach leaves	250 mL
2	Gala apples, thinly sliced	2
4 oz	smoked Gouda cheese, cut into thin slices	125 g

1. Brush one side of each bread slice with butter. Place on a work surface, buttered side down. Spread 4 bread slices equally with mayonnaise. Top equally with chicken, spinach, apples and cheese. Cover with remaining bread slices, buttered side up, and press together gently.

2. Place sandwiches on preheated panini grill or in a large skillet over medium heat and cook, turning once if using a skillet, for 3 to 4 minutes or until golden brown and cheese is melted. Serve immediately.

Grilled Chicken, Tomatoes and Olives

Serves 4

This sandwich is a take off of a chicken dish I cook in a skillet or a grill pan. It makes a wonderful grilled cheese that's sure to please.

Tip

If you're cooking your own chicken for this sandwich, season 1½ lbs (750 g) boneless skinless chicken breasts with ½ to 1 tsp (2 to 5 mL) chipotle seasoning, depending on your heat preference.

- Panini grill or large skillet
- Preheat panini grill to medium, if using

8	slices sourdough bread (½-inch/1 cm thick slices)	8
2 tbsp	butter or margarine, softened	30 mL
¼ cup	Homemade Mayonnaise (page 188) or store-bought or Chipotle Aïoli (page 190)	60 mL
8 oz	thinly sliced cooked chicken (see Tip, left)	250 g
8	slices Swiss cheese	8
2	tomatoes, thinly sliced	2
1 cup	sliced black olives	250 mL

1. Brush one side of each bread slice with butter. Place on a work surface, buttered side down. Spread 4 bread slices equally with mayonnaise. Top equally with chicken, cheese, tomatoes and olives. Cover with remaining bread slices, buttered side up, and press together gently.

2. Place sandwiches on preheated panini grill or in a large skillet over medium heat and cook, turning once if using a skillet, for 3 to 4 minutes or until golden brown and cheese is melted. Serve immediately.

Grilled Southern Barbecue Sandwich

Serves 4

I make these all the time, and they are just as good as the ones served in Southern barbecue restaurants.

- **Panini grill or large skillet**
- **Preheat panini grill to medium, if using**

8	slices sourdough bread (½-inch/1 cm thick slices)	8
¼ cup	butter or margarine, softened	60 mL
¼ cup	Barbecue Sauce (page 192) or store-bought	60 mL
2 cups	thinly sliced cooked chicken	500 mL
4	slices mozzarella cheese	4
½ cup	sliced dill pickles	125 mL

1. Brush one side of each bread slice with butter. Place on a work surface, buttered side down. Spread 4 bread slices equally with barbecue sauce. Top equally with chicken, cheese and pickles. Cover with remaining bread slices, buttered side up, and press together gently.

2. Place sandwiches on preheated panini grill or in a large skillet over medium heat and cook, turning once if using a skillet, for 3 to 4 minutes or until golden brown and cheese is melted. Serve immediately.

Grilled Tequila Citrus Panini

Serves 4	

This sandwich was inspired by a tequila chicken recipe I like. Serve it with chips, salsa and guacamole.

Tips

You can omit the tequila if you want. Use the same amounts for orange juice and lime juice.

You can also broil chicken. Place on a baking sheet, lined with parchment paper. Broil chicken, turning once, for 4 to 6 minutes per side or until chicken is no longer pink inside.

- **Preheat greased barbecue grill to medium-high**
- **Panini grill or large skillet**
- **Preheat panini grill to medium, if using**

¼ cup	tequila (see Tips, left)	60 mL
¼ cup	freshly squeezed orange juice	60 mL
¼ cup	freshly squeezed lime juice	60 mL
2 tsp	chili powder	10 mL
1	clove garlic, minced	1
1 tsp	salt	5 mL
1 tsp	freshly ground black pepper	5 mL
4	boneless skinless chicken cutlets, about 1½ lbs (750 g) total (see Tips, left)	4
8	slices sourdough bread (½-inch/1 cm thick slices)	8
2 tbsp	olive oil	30 mL
4	slices Monterey Jack cheese	4

1. In a shallow dish, combine tequila, orange juice, lime juice, chili powder, garlic, salt and pepper. Add chicken, turning to coat. Cover and marinate in the refrigerator for at least 2 hours.

2. Remove chicken from marinade. Discard marinade. Grill chicken on preheated grill or panini grill for 4 minutes per side or until chicken is no longer pink inside.

3. Brush one side of each bread slice with olive oil. Place on a work surface, oiled side down. Top 4 bread slices equally with chicken cutlets and cheese. Cover with remaining bread slices, oiled side up, and press together gently.

4. Place sandwiches on preheated panini grill or in a large skillet over medium heat and cook, turning once if using a skillet, for 3 to 4 minutes or until golden brown and cheese is melted. Serve immediately.

Lemon Basil Chicken Panini

Serves 4

This chicken is my daughter's favorite. When I made it as a grilled cheese, it was an instant hit.

Tips

You can also broil chicken. Place on a baking sheet, lined with parchment paper. Broil chicken, turning once, for 4 to 6 minutes per side or until chicken is no longer pink inside.

I love using chicken cutlets because they are thinner and cook so much more quickly than chicken breasts.

- Preheat greased barbecue grill to medium
- Panini grill or large skillet
- Preheat panini grill to medium-high, if using

1/4 cup	olive oil, divided	60 mL
1/3 cup	freshly squeezed lemon juice	75 mL
2	cloves garlic, minced	2
1 tbsp	chopped fresh basil	15 mL
1 tbsp	chopped fresh rosemary	15 mL
1/4 tsp	kosher salt	1 mL
1/4 tsp	freshly ground black pepper	1 mL
4	boneless skinless chicken cutlets (about 1 1/2 lbs/750 g total) (see Tips, left)	4
8	slices Italian bread (1/2-inch/1 cm thick slices)	8
1/3 cup	freshly grated Parmesan cheese	75 mL

1. In a small bowl, combine 2 tbsp (30 mL) of the olive oil, lemon juice, garlic, basil, rosemary, salt and pepper. Place chicken in a large bowl and pour marinade over chicken and marinate for at least 30 minutes or for up to 8 hours in the refrigerator.

2. Remove chicken from marinade and discard marinade. Grill chicken on preheated grill or panini grill for 4 minutes per side or until chicken is no longer pink inside. Set aside.

3. Brush one side of each bread slice with remaining olive oil. Place on a work surface, oiled side down. Top 4 bread slices equally with chicken and cheese. Top with remaining bread slices, oiled side up, and press together gently.

4. Place sandwiches on preheated panini grill or in a large skillet over medium heat and cook, turning once if using a skillet, for 3 to 4 minutes or until golden brown and cheese is melted. Serve immediately.

Grilled Chicken Gremolata Sandwich

Serves 4

Gremolata is a paste made of herbs, garlic and citrus often found in Italy.

Tips

You can also broil chicken. Place on a baking sheet, lined with foil. Broil chicken, turning once, for 4 to 6 minutes per side or until chicken is no longer pink inside.

If you have leftover grilled chicken on hand, feel free to use that in this sandwich.

- Preheat lightly greased barbecue grill to medium-high
- Panini grill or large skillet
- Preheat panini grill to medium, if using

¼ cup	chopped fresh parsley	60 mL
2 tbsp	grated lemon zest	30 mL
2	cloves garlic, minced	2
1½ tsp	dried Italian seasoning	7 mL
1 tsp	sea salt, divided	5 mL
8 tbsp	olive oil, divided	120 mL
¼ cup	freshly squeezed lemon juice	60 mL
4	boneless skinless chicken cutlets, about 1½ lbs (750 g)	4
¼ tsp	freshly ground black pepper	1 mL
8	ciabatta or Italian bread (½-inch/1 cm thick slices), toasted	8
4	slices mozzarella cheese	4

1. In a small bowl, combine parsley, lemon zest, garlic, Italian seasoning and ½ tsp (2 mL) of the salt. Stir in 6 tbsp (90 mL) of the olive oil. Set aside.

2. Drizzle lemon juice over chicken and season with remaining salt and pepper. Cook chicken on preheated grill or panini grill for 4 minutes per side or until chicken is no longer pink inside. Set aside.

3. Brush one side of each bread slice with remaining 2 tbsp (30 mL) olive oil. Place on a work surface, oiled side down. Spread 4 bread slices with parsley mixture. Top 4 bread slices equally with chicken and cheese. Press together gently, oiled side up.

4. Place sandwiches on preheated grill, panini grill or in a skillet and cook, turning once if using a skillet, for 3 to 4 minutes or until golden brown and cheese is melted. Serve immediately.

Chicken Pesto Panini

Serves 4

This chicken pesto panini sandwich makes an easy weeknight dinner or fun weekend entertaining recipe, especially in the summer when basil is plentiful.

Tips

If you don't have time to make the pesto, you can use store-bought pesto.

I like to use chicken cutlets because they are thinner and cook quicker. Or, you can slice your chicken breasts lengthwise in half for thinner pieces.

- **Food processor**

Walnut Pesto (see Tips, left)

1/2 cup	fresh basil leaves	125 mL
1/4 cup	chopped walnuts	60 mL
1	clove garlic, minced	1
1 tsp	freshly squeezed lemon juice	5 mL
1/2 tsp	kosher salt, divided	2 mL
1/3 cup + 1 tbsp	olive oil, divided	90 mL
4	boneless skinless chicken cutlets (about 1 lb/500 g total) (see Tips, left)	4
1/4 tsp	ground oregano	1 mL
1/4 tsp	garlic powder	1 mL
1/4 tsp	freshly ground black pepper	1 mL
8	slices sourdough bread (1/2-inch/1 cm thick) slices)	8
1/4 cup	butter, melted	60 mL
1/2 cup	shredded Parmesan cheese	125 mL

1. *Walnut Pesto:* In a food processor, combine basil, walnuts, garlic, lemon juice and 1/4 tsp (1 mL) of the salt. With motor running, add 1/3 cup (75 mL) of the olive oil through the feed hole until combined. Set aside.

2. Season chicken with oregano, garlic powder, pepper and remaining 1/4 tsp (1 mL) salt. In a large skillet, heat 1 tbsp (15 mL) of remaining oil over medium-high heat. Add chicken and cook for 4 minutes per side or until tender and no longer pink inside. Remove from skillet and set aside. Wipe skillet clean.

3. Brush one side of each bread slice with butter. Place on a work surface, buttered side down. Spread 4 slices equally with pesto. Top equally with chicken and cheese. Cover with remaining bread slices, buttered side up, and press together gently.

4. Place sandwiches on a large skillet over medium heat and cook, turning once, for 3 to 4 minutes or until golden brown and cheese is melted. Serve immediately.

Chicken-Provolone Sandwich

Serves 4

The secret ingredient in this sandwich is the red wine vinaigrette.

Tips

The best way to clean fresh mushrooms is with a mushroom brush or damp paper towel right before using.

Baby bella mushrooms look like button mushrooms but are mini immature portobello mushrooms that have more flavor than button mushrooms. They are often found in the produce section of the grocery store where the other mushrooms are sold.

You can also broil chicken. Place on a baking sheet, lined with parchment paper. Broil chicken, turning once, for 4 to 6 minutes per side or until chicken is no longer pink inside.

- **Panini grill or large skillet**
- **Preheat panini grill to medium, if using**

½ cup	red wine vinaigrette, divided	125 mL
4	boneless skinless chicken cutlets (about 1½ lbs/ 750 g total) (see Tips, left)	4
¾ cup	sliced baby bella mushrooms (see Tips, left)	175 mL
½ cup	diced red onion	125 mL
4	slices French bread (½-inch/ 1 cm thick slices), cut in half diagonally	4
2 tbsp	olive oil	30 mL
1 cup	romaine lettuce leaves	250 mL
1	avocado, sliced	1
4	provolone cheese slices	4

1. In a shallow dish or resealable plastic bag, combine ¼ cup (60 mL) of the vinaigrette and chicken, coating evenly. Cover and refrigerate for 15 minutes. Drain and discard marinade.

2. Brush mushrooms and red onion with remaining vinaigrette. Set aside.

3. In a large skillet, cook chicken for 6 minutes per side or until no longer pink inside.

4. In skillet over medium heat, cook mushrooms and red onions, stirring frequently, for 4 minutes or until onions are softened.

5. Brush one side of each bread slice with olive oil. Place on a work surface, oiled side down. Top 4 bread slices equally with chicken, lettuce, mushroom mixture, avocado and cheese. Cover with remaining bread slices, oiled side up, and press together gently.

6. Place sandwiches on preheated panini grill or in a large skillet over medium-high heat and cook, turning once if using a skillet, for 3 to 4 minutes or until golden brown and cheese is melted. Serve immediately.

Grilled Feta and Turkey

This Greek-style grilled cheese is very unique. Feel free to substitute ham, roast beef or any deli meats for the turkey in this recipe.

- Panini grill or large skillet
- Preheat panini grill to medium, if using

8	slices Italian bread (1/2-inch/1 cm thick slices)	8
1/4 cup	butter or margarine, softened	60 mL
1/4 cup	Red Pepper Hummus (page 186) or store-bought	60 mL
12 oz	thinly sliced deli turkey	375 g
4	slices provolone cheese	4
4 oz	crumbled feta cheese (see Tips, page 162)	125 g
1 cup	fresh spinach leaves	250 mL

1. Brush one side of each bread slice with butter. Place on a work surface, buttered side down. Spread 4 bread slices equally with Red Pepper Hummus. Top equally with turkey, provolone, feta and spinach. Cover with remaining bread slices, buttered side up, and press together gently.

2. Place sandwiches on preheated panini grill or in a large skillet over medium heat and cook, turning once if using a skillet, for 3 to 4 minutes or until golden brown and cheese is melted. Serve immediately.

Hawaiian Grilled Cheese

Serves 4

It's fun to make these sandwiches in the wintertime because they always feel like summer.

Tips

I love to grill the pineapple to put on these sandwiches. Grill over medium-high heat for 1 to 2 minutes or until grill marks appear.

If you can't find Hawaiian bread, use any small rolls.

- **Panini grill or large skillet**
- **Preheat panini grill to medium, if using**

8	slices Hawaiian bread or 4 rolls (see Tip, left)	8
2 tbsp	olive oil	30 mL
4 tsp	liquid honey	20 mL
8 oz	thinly sliced turkey	250 g
4	slices Monterey Jack cheese	4
1 cup	pineapple slices	250 mL
4	leafy lettuce leaves	4

1. Brush one side of each bread slice with oil. Place on a work surface, oiled side down. Spread bottom halves equally with honey. Top equally with turkey, cheese, pineapple and lettuce. Cover with remaining bread slices, oiled side up, and press together gently.

2. Place sandwiches on preheated panini grill or in a large skillet over medium heat and cook, turning once if using a skillet, for 3 to 4 minutes or until golden brown and cheese is melted. Serve immediately.

Turkey Antipasto Grilled Cheese

This Italian-style sandwich has a delicious mixture of meats, cheese and vegetables. It's not only great tasting but also pretty and colorful.

- **Panini grill or large skillet**
- **Preheat panini grill to medium, if using**

8	slices Italian bread (1/2-inch/1 cm thick slices	8
2 tbsp	olive oil	30 mL
4 oz	thinly sliced turkey	125 g
4 oz	thinly sliced Italian salami	125 g
2	slices provolone cheese	2
2	slices fontina cheese	2
3/4 cup	roasted red peppers	175 mL
1/2 cup	chopped kalamata olives	125 mL

1. Brush one side of each bread slice with olive oil. Place on a work surface, oiled side down. Top 4 bread slices equally with turkey, salami and provolone and fontina cheeses. Arrange red peppers and olives equally on top. Cover with remaining bread slices, oiled side up, and press together gently.

2. Place sandwiches on preheated panini grill or in a large skillet over medium heat and cook, turning once if using a skillet, for 3 to 4 minutes or until golden brown and cheese is melted. Serve immediately.

Variation

Substitute mozzarella cheese for the fontina or just double the amount of provolone.

Grilled Turkey Cobb

I love Cobb salad, and turkey, bacon, spinach, blue cheese and mozzarella make a delicious grilled cheese sandwich.

- Panini grill or large skillet
- Preheat panini grill to medium, if using

8	slices white or whole wheat bread (1/2-inch/1 cm thick slices)	8
1/4 cup	olive oil	60 mL
6 oz	thinly sliced turkey	175 g
1 cup	fresh baby spinach leaves	250 mL
8	slices cooked bacon	8
2	tomatoes, thinly sliced	2
2	avocados, sliced	2
4	slices mozzarella cheese	4
1/2 cup	crumbled blue cheese	125 mL

1. Brush one side of each bread slice with olive oil. Place on a work surface, oiled side down. Top 4 bread slices equally with turkey, spinach, bacon, tomato slices, avocado, mozzarella and blue cheese. Cover with remaining bread slices, oiled side up, and press together gently.

2. Place sandwiches on preheated panini grill or in a large skillet over medium heat and cook, turning once if using a skillet, for 3 to 4 minutes or until golden brown and cheese is melted. Serve immediately.

Variation

To make this sandwich lower in fat, try turkey bacon. It isn't as crisp but tastes great.

Grilled Turkey and Brie with Apricot

Serves 4

This sandwich is wonderfully sweet and savory because the Brie and Granny Smith apple pair so well together.

Tip

Apples ripen quickly so be sure to store them in the coldest part of the refrigerator if you're not going to eat them for a while.

- **Panini grill or large skillet**
- **Preheat panini grill to medium, if using**

8	slices sourdough bread (1/2-inch/1 cm thick slices)	8
2 tbsp	butter or margarine, softened	30 mL
1/2 cup	apricot preserves or jam	125 mL
8 oz	thinly sliced maple-glazed turkey	250 g
4 oz	Brie, sliced	125 g
2	medium Granny Smith apples, thinly sliced (see Tip, left)	2

1. Brush one side of each bread slice with butter. Place 4 slices on a work surface, buttered side down. Spread remaining 4 bread slices equally with apricot preserves. Top equally with turkey, Brie and apples. Cover with remaining bread slices, buttered side up, and press together gently.

2. Place sandwiches on preheated panini grill or in a large skillet over medium heat and cook, turning once if using a skillet, for 3 to 4 minutes or until golden brown and cheese is melted. Serve immediately.

Turkey-Havarti Grinder

Serves 4

Other names of this sandwich are Po' Boy, Cuban, Torpedo and Zep. Whatever the name, this version is good.

- **Panini grill or large skillet**
- **Preheat panini grill to medium, if using**

1/3 cup	Dijon mustard	75 mL
2 tbsp	Homemade Mayonnaise (page 188) or store-bought	30 mL
1/8 tsp	hot pepper flakes	0.5 mL
8	slices French bread (1/2-inch/1 cm thick slices)	8
2 tbsp	butter or margarine, softened	30 mL
1 lb	thinly sliced turkey	500 g
2 cups	fresh spinach leaves	500 mL
2	small tomatoes, thinly sliced	2
4	sweet pickle slices	4
2 oz	Havarti cheese, thinly sliced	60 g

1. In a small bowl, combine mustard, mayonnaise and hot pepper flakes.

2. Brush one side of each bread slice with butter. Place on a work surface, buttered side down. Spread 4 bread slices equally with mayonnaise mixture. Top equally with turkey, spinach, tomatoes, pickles and cheese. Cover with remaining bread slices, buttered side up, and press together gently.

3. Place sandwiches on preheated panini grill or in a large skillet over medium-high heat and cook, turning once if using a skillet, for 3 to 4 minutes or until golden brown and cheese is melted. Serve immediately.

Variation

You can omit the sweet pickles or use fresh dill.

Turkey-Jalapeño Melt

This is a great recipe to use up your leftover turkey. Spice it up even more by using Monterey Jack cheese with jalapeño peppers.

Tip

You can find pickled jalapeño peppers in the ethnic section of the grocery store where Mexican foods are sold.

- **Panini grill or large skillet**
- **Preheat panini grill to medium, if using**

8	slices sourdough bread (1/2-inch/1 cm thick slices)	8
2 tbsp	canola or olive oil	30 mL
1/4 cup	Chipotle Aïoli (page 190) or store-bought mayonnaise	60 mL
12 oz	thinly sliced roasted turkey	375 g
2	medium tomatoes, sliced thinly, seeds removed	2
1/4 cup	sliced pickled jalapeño peppers (see Tips, left)	60 mL
4	slices Monterey Jack cheese	4

1. Brush one side of each bread slice with oil. Place on a work surface, oiled side down. Spread 4 bread slices equally with Chipotle Aïoli. Top equally with turkey, tomatoes, peppers and cheese. Cover with remaining bread slices, oiled side up and press together gently.

2. Place sandwiches on preheated panini grill or in a large skillet over medium heat and cook, turning once if using a skillet, for 3 to 4 minutes or until golden brown and cheese is melted. Serve immediately.

Variation

This also works great with leftover ham or grilled chicken slices and Cheddar or Colby Jack cheese instead of Monterey Jack.

Grilled Turkey Tenderloin Sandwich

Serves 4

The balsamic and brown sugar sauce goes great on this turkey sandwich topped with provolone cheese.

- Preheat greased barbecue grill to medium
- Panini grill or large skillet
- Preheat panini grill to medium, if using

5 tbsp	olive oil, divided	75 mL
1/2 cup	chopped onion	125 mL
1 cup	balsamic vinegar	250 mL
1 tbsp	tomato paste	15 mL
1/4 cup	packed brown sugar	60 mL
1 tbsp	Worcestershire sauce	15 mL
1 tbsp	Dijon mustard	15 mL
4	turkey tenderloins (about 1 1/2 lbs/750 g total)	4
1/4 tsp	salt	1 mL
1/4 tsp	freshly ground black pepper	1 mL
8	slices Italian bread (1/2-inch/1 cm thick slices)	8
4	slices provolone cheese	4

1. In a medium skillet, heat 2 tbsp (30 mL) of the olive oil over medium heat. Add onion and cook, stirring frequently, for about 5 minutes or until softened. Add vinegar, tomato paste, brown sugar, Worcestershire sauce and Dijon mustard. Increase heat to medium-high. Bring to a boil. Reduce heat and simmer for about 10 minutes or until reduced by half. Set aside.

2. Sprinkle tenderloins with salt and pepper and drizzle with 1 tbsp (15 mL) of olive oil. Separate 3 tbsp (45 mL) of the vinegar mixture and brush on turkey. Grill turkey on preheated grill for 4 minutes per side or until no longer pink inside.

3. Brush one side of each bread slice with remaining 2 tbsp (30 mL) of olive oil. Place bread on a work surface, oiled side down. Spread 4 bread slices equally with remaining vinegar mixture. Top equally with turkey and cheese. Cover with remaining bread slices, oiled side up, and press together gently.

4. Place sandwiches on preheated grill, panini grill or in a skillet and cook, turning once if using a skillet, for 3 to 4 minutes or until golden brown and cheese is melted. Serve immediately.

Variation

Substitute chicken cutlets or thinly sliced pork tenderloin for the turkey tenderloins.

Pork

Grilled Ham, Goat Cheese and Figs

Serves 4

This grilled cheese has a terrific mix of sweet and savory flavors.

Tip

One pound (500 g) fresh figs yields about 2 cups (500 mL) chopped. Figs are usually available June through October. If you can't find fresh figs or they're not in season, substitute dried.

- **Panini grill or large skillet**
- **Preheat panini grill to medium, if using**

8	slices Italian bread (1/2 -inch/1 cm thick slices)	8
1/4 cup	butter or margarine, softened	60 mL
1/4 cup	liquid honey	60 mL
12 oz	thinly sliced ham or turkey	375 g
1 cup	baby spinach leaves	250 mL
1 1/2 cups	chopped figs	375 mL
4 oz	crumbled goat cheese	125 g

1. Brush one side of each bread slice with butter. Place on a work surface, buttered side down. Spread 4 bread slices equally with honey. Top equally with ham, spinach, figs and cheese. Cover with remaining bread slices, buttered side up, and press together gently.

2. Place sandwiches on preheated panini grill or in a large skillet over medium heat and cook, turning once if using a skillet, for 3 to 4 minutes or until golden brown and cheese is melted. Serve immediately.

Mini Grilled Cheese with Marinara

This makes a great appetizer recipe or a fun way to serve grilled cheese for a main dish as well.

Tip

I use jarred marinara sauce in this recipe to save time.

- Panini grill or large skillet
- Preheat panini grill to medium, if using

8	slices French, white or multigrain bread (½-inch/1 cm thick slices)	8
¼ cup	butter or margarine, softened	60 mL
¼ cup	Homemade Mayonnaise (page 188) or store-bought	60 mL
6 oz	thinly sliced ham	175 g
6 oz	thinly sliced roast beef	175 g
3 oz	sliced pepperoni	90 g
¾ cup	fresh basil leaves	175 mL
4	slices provolone or mozzarella	4
1 cup	marinara sauce, warmed (see Tip, left)	250 mL

1. Brush one side of each bread slice with butter. Place on a work surface, buttered side down. Spread 4 bread slices equally with mayonnaise. Top equally with ham, roast beef, pepperoni, basil and cheese. Cover with remaining bread slices, buttered side up, and press together gently.

2. Place sandwiches on preheated panini grill or in a large skillet over medium heat and cook, turning once if using a skillet, for 3 to 4 minutes or until golden brown and cheese is melted. Cut each sandwich into thirds. Serve immediately with warmed marinara.

Ham and Gouda Melts

Serves 4

The buttery, nutty flavor of Gouda pairs well with the ham in this hot sandwich. I call this a "comfort food" sandwich.

Tip

If you have leftover ham, it works great instead of the deli sliced.

- **Panini grill or large skillet**
- **Preheated panini grill to medium, if using**

8	slices country white or sourdough bread (½-inch/1 cm thick slices)	8
2 tbsp	butter or margarine, softened	30 mL
¼ cup	Homemade Mayonnaise (page 188) or store-bought	60 mL
12 oz	thinly sliced ham	375 g
1 cup	chopped mixed greens	250 mL
4 oz	Gouda cheese, thinly sliced	125 g

1. Brush one side of each bread slice with butter. Place on a work surface, buttered side down. Spread 4 bread slices equally with mayonnaise. Top equally with ham, greens and Gouda. Cover with remaining bread slices, buttered side up, and press together gently.

2. Place sandwiches on preheated panini grill or in a large skillet over medium heat and cook, turning once if using a skillet, for 3 to 4 minutes or until golden brown and cheese is melted. Serve immediately.

Black Russian

This idea came to me from a New York friend who said she used to eat this often as a cold sandwich. Either way, I love the rustic combination of ingredients.

Tip

You can substitute regular Brie for the cracked pepper one.

- **Panini grill or large skillet**
- **Preheat panini grill to medium, if using**

½ cup	stone-ground mustard	125 mL
1 tbsp	chopped fresh parsley	15 mL
1 tsp	grated lemon zest	5 mL
8	slices pumpernickel bread (½-inch/1 cm thick slices)	8
¼ cup	olive oil	60 mL
8 oz	Black Forest ham	250 g
1 cup	lettuce leaves	250 mL
4 oz	cracked pepper Brie (see Tip, left)	125 g

1. In a small bowl, combine mustard, parsley and lemon zest.

2. Brush one side of each bread slice with olive oil. Place on a work surface, oiled side down. Spread bread slices equally with mustard mixture. Top 4 slices equally with ham, lettuce and Brie. Cover with remaining bread slices, oiled side up, and press together gently.

3. Place sandwiches on preheated panini grill or in a large skillet over medium heat and cook, turning once if using a skillet, for 3 to 4 minutes or until golden brown and cheese is melted. Serve immediately.

Grilled Ham and Jarlsberg on Brioche

Serves 4

This recipe was shared by my friend, Kelley, who is a personal chef in Park City, Utah. Her blog is at http:// mountainmamacooks. com. When she told me, "This was so good that I almost cried," I knew I had to have this recipe in my book.

Tip

Brioche bread is an egg-type, sweet, rich bread and can be found in most gourmet grocery stores. If you can't find it, substitute challah bread.

- **Panini grill or large skillet**
- **Preheat panini grill to medium, if using**

2 tsp	Dijon mustard	10 mL
4 tbsp	peach preserves or jam	60 mL
8	slices brioche bread (½-inch/1 cm thick slices) (see Tip, left)	8
4 tbsp	butter, softened	60 mL
8 to 10	slices leftover spiral-cut ham (about 8 oz/250 g) or thick-sliced deli ham	8 to 10
1 cup	grated Jarlsberg cheese	250 mL

1. In a small bowl, combine Dijon mustard and peach preserves, stirring until completely combined. Set aside.

2. Brush one side of each bread slice with butter. Place on a work surface, buttered side down. Spread 4 bread slices equally with Dijon mixture. Top equally with ham and Jarlsberg. Cover with remaining bread slices, buttered side up, and press together gently.

3. Place sandwiches on a preheated panini grill or in a large skillet over medium heat and cook, turning once if using a skillet, for 3 to 4 minutes or until golden brown and cheese is melted. Serve immediately.

Southern-Style Grilled Cheese

Serves 4

This southern twist on a grilled cheese is perfect to serve on New Year's Day when supposedly eating greens brings luck for the new year.

Tip

To cook collards: In a skillet over medium heat, combine 1 tbsp (15 mL) oil, 1 clove minced garlic, 2 tbsp (30 mL) chopped red onion, ¼ tsp (1 mL) salt and ¼ tsp (1 mL) black pepper and cook for 3 minutes or until garlic and onion are tender. Add collards and cook for 5 minutes more or until slightly wilted and tender.

- **Panini grill or large skillet**
- **Preheat panini grill to medium, if using**

8	slices sourdough (½-inch/1 cm thick slices)	8
2 tbsp	butter, softened	30 mL
4 tbsp	Homemade Mayonnaise (page 188) or store-bought	60 mL
8	slices bacon, cooked	8
1 cup	cooked collard greens, drained (see Tip, left)	250 mL
2	tomatoes, thinly sliced	2
4 oz	Swiss cheese slices	125 g
4 oz	provolone slices	125 g

1. Brush one side of each bread slice with butter. Place on a work surface, buttered sided down. Spread 4 bread slices equally with mayonnaise. Top equally with bacon, collards, tomatoes and Swiss and provolone cheeses. Cover with remaining bread slices, buttered side up, and press together gently.

2. Place sandwiches on preheated panini grill or in a large skillet over medium heat and cook, turning once if using a skillet, for 3 to 4 minutes or until golden brown and cheese is melted. Serve immediately.

Variation

Substitute leftover sliced pork for the bacon in this recipe.

Grilled Applewood Smoked Bacon and Almonds

Serves 4

I love the apple flavor from smoked bacon paired with cheese in this sandwich.

Tips

Look for applewood smoked bacon where bacon is sold in the grocery store.

Feel free to omit the nuts, if desired.

- **Panini grill or large skillet**
- **Preheat panini grill to medium, if using**

8	slices brioche (1/2-inch/1 cm thick slices)	8
2 tbsp	butter or margarine, softened	30 mL
1/4 cup	liquid honey	60 mL
8	slices smoked bacon, preferably Applewood (see Tips, left)	8
8 oz	deli sliced ham	250 g
4 oz	Muenster cheese, cut into 4 slices	125 g
3/4 cup	chopped almonds, toasted	175 mL

1. Brush one side of each bread slice with butter. Place on a work surface, buttered side down. Spread 4 bread slices equally with honey. Top equally with bacon, ham, cheese and almonds. Cover with remaining bread slices, buttered side up, and press together gently.

2. Place sandwiches on preheated panini grill or in a large skillet over medium heat and cook, turning once if using a skillet, for 3 to 4 minutes or until golden brown and cheese is melted. Serve immediately.

Grilled Spinach, Pepper Jack and Bacon

Serves 4	

I love the spice of pepper Jack cheese with the bacon in this grilled cheese. It's perfect for a weeknight dinner.

- Panini grill or large skillet
- Preheat panini grill to medium, if using

8	slices multigrain ($1/2$-inch/1 cm thick slices)	8
2 tbsp	butter or margarine, softened	30 mL
$1/2$ cup	Basil Pesto (page 181) or store-bought	125 mL
8	slices cooked bacon	8
4	slices pepper Jack cheese	4
$1^1/_2$ cups	baby spinach leaves	375 mL

1. Brush one side of each bread slice with butter. Place on a work surface, buttered side down. Spread tops of bread slices equally with pesto. Top 4 slices equally with bacon, cheese and spinach. Cover with remaining bread slices, buttered side up, and press together gently.

2. Place sandwiches on preheated panini grill or in a large skillet over medium heat and cook, turning once if using a skillet, for 3 to 4 minutes or until golden brown and cheese is melted. Serve immediately.

BLT Grilled Cheese with Avocado

I get a great response whenever I make this sandwich. These are all of my favorite ingredients tied into one great recipe.

- **Panini grill or large skillet**
- **Preheat panini grill to medium, if using**

8	slices Italian bread (½-inch/1 cm thick slices)	8
2 tbsp	butter or margarine, softened	30 mL
¼ cup	Homemade Mayonnaise (page 188) or store-bought	60 mL
2	avocados, thinly sliced	2
8	slices cooked bacon	8
2	tomatoes, thinly sliced	2
4 oz	mozzarella cheese, thinly sliced	125 g

1. Brush one side of each bread slice with butter. Place on a work surface, buttered side down. Spread 4 bread slices equally with mayonnaise. Top equally with bacon, tomatoes, avocados and cheese. Cover with remaining bread slices, buttered side up, and press together gently.

2. Place sandwiches on preheated panini grill or in a large skillet over medium heat and cook, turning once if using a skillet, for 3 to 4 minutes or until golden brown and cheese is melted. Serve immediately.

Grilled Pimiento Cheese BLT

These delicious sandwiches are a Southern favorite. You can't go wrong with warmed pimiento cheese slightly melted on sourdough bread.

Tip

Be sure to butter the bread, not the skillet, when making grilled sandwiches.

- **Panini grill or large skillet**
- **Preheat panini grill to medium, if using**

8	slices sourdough bread (1/2-inch/1 cm thick slices)	8
4 tbsp	butter or margarine, softened (see Tip, left)	60 mL
2 cups	Pimiento Cheese (page 193) or store-bought	500 mL
8	lettuce leaves	8
8	slices cooked bacon	8
1	large tomato, cut into 8 slices	1

1. Brush one side of each bread slice with butter. Place on a work surface, buttered side down. Top 4 bread slices equally with Pimiento Cheese, lettuce, bacon and tomato. Cover with remaining bread slices, buttered side up, and press together gently.

2. Place sandwiches on preheated panini grill or in a large skillet over medium heat and cook, turning once if using a skillet, for 3 to 4 minutes or until golden brown and cheese is melted. Serve immediately.

Grilled Pimiento Cheese with Bacon and Pickles

This sandwich was crafted by my assistant, Alatia. It's a true family favorite.

Tip

This sandwich is also good served with lettuce and tomato after it's cooked.

- Panini grill or large skillet
- Preheat panini grill to medium, if using

8	slices sourdough bread (½-inch/1 cm thick slices)	8
¼ cup	butter or margarine, softened	60 mL
1 cup	Pimiento Cheese (page 193) or store-bought	250 mL
1½ cups	small dill pickles	375 mL
8	slices cooked bacon	8

1. Brush one side of each bread slice with butter. Place on a work surface, buttered side down. Top 4 bread slices equally with Pimiento Cheese, pickles and bacon. Cover with remaining bread slices, buttered side up, and press together gently.

2. Place sandwiches on preheated panini grill or in a large skillet over medium heat and cook, turning once if using a skillet, for 3 to 4 minutes or until golden brown and cheese is melted. Serve immediately.

Grilled Bacon and Fried Green Tomatoes

Serves 4

It doesn't get more Southern than this. I make these on very special occasions.

Tip

If you can't find green tomatoes, feel free to use fresh tomatoes and omit the frying step.

- Panini grill or large skillet
- Preheat panini grill to medium, if using

1/4 cup	self-rising cornmeal	60 mL
2 tbsp	all-purpose flour	30 mL
2 tbsp	panko bread crumbs	30 mL
1/4 tsp	salt	1 mL
1/4 tsp	freshly ground black pepper	1 mL
2	green tomatoes, thinly sliced (see Tip, left)	2
1/3 cup	olive oil	75 mL
8	slices sourdough bread (1/2-inch/1 cm thick slices)	8
1/4 cup	butter or margarine, softened	60 mL
1/4 cup	Homemade Mayonnaise (page 188) or store-bought	60 mL
8	slices cooked bacon	8
4	slices Cheddar cheese	4

1. In a small bowl, combine cornmeal, flour, bread crumbs, salt and pepper. Coat green tomatoes with cornmeal mixture.

2. In a large skillet, heat oil over medium heat. Add tomatoes and cook for 5 minutes per side or until lightly browned.

3. Brush one side of each bread slice with butter. Place on a work surface, buttered side down. Spread 4 bread slices equally with mayonnaise. Top equally with bacon, tomatoes and cheese. Cover with remaining bread slices, buttered side up, and press together gently.

4. Place sandwiches on preheated panini grill or in a large skillet over medium heat and cook, turning once if using a skillet, for 3 to 4 minutes or until golden brown and cheese is melted. Serve immediately.

Grilled Gourmet Pimiento Cheese

When someone asked me how to make a gourmet grilled cheese, I told them to add white Cheddar, fresh watercress and prosciutto.

Tips

Shred Cheddar cheese by hand or by using a food processor. If you're using hard cheese, such as Parmesan, let it get to room temperature before grating.

The pimiento cheese can be stored, covered and refrigerated, for up to 3 days.

- **Panini grill or large skillet**
- **Preheat panini grill to medium, if using**

Pimiento Cheese

¼ cup	Homemade Mayonnaise (page 188) or store-bought	60 mL
2 tbsp	finely chopped red onion	30 mL
4 oz	diced pimientos, drained	125 g
⅛ tsp	cayenne pepper	0.5 mL
4 oz	shredded sharp (aged) Cheddar cheese (see Tip, left)	125 g
4 oz	shredded white Cheddar	125 g
8	slices Italian bread (½-inch/1 cm thick slices)	8
¼ cup	butter or margarine, softened	60 mL
8 oz	thinly sliced prosciutto	250 g
1⅓ cups	watercress	325 mL

1. *Pimiento Cheese:* In a medium bowl, combine mayonnaise, red onion, pimientos and cayenne. Gently stir in sharp and white Cheddar cheeses.

2. Brush one side of each bread slice with butter. Place on a work surface, buttered side down. Top 4 bread slices equally with Pimiento Cheese, prosciutto and watercress. Cover with remaining bread slices, buttered side up, and press together gently.

3. Place sandwiches on preheated panini grill or in a large skillet over medium heat and cook, turning once if using a skillet, for 3 to 4 minutes or until golden brown and cheese is melted. Serve immediately.

Prosciutto and Fontina Grilled Cheese

I call this a "dressy" grilled cheese. It's definitely for special occasions and also works well as an appetizer.

- **Panini grill or large skillet**
- **Preheat panini grill to medium, if using**

8	slices Italian bread (½-inch/1 cm thick slices)	8
¼ cup	olive oil	60 mL
¼ cup	Basil Pesto (page 181) or store-bought	60 mL
8 oz	thinly sliced prosciutto	250 g
1 cup	arugula leaves	125 mL
4	slices fontina cheese	4

1. Brush one side of each bread slice with olive oil. Place on a work surface, oiled side down. Spread 4 bread slices equally with pesto. Top equally with prosciutto, arugula leaves and fontina. Cover with remaining bread slices, oiled side up, and press together gently.

2. Place sandwiches on preheated panini grill or in a large skillet over medium heat and cook, turning once if using a skillet, for 3 to 4 minutes or until golden brown and cheese is melted. Serve immediately.

Prosciutto-Feta Grilled Cheese

This grilled cheese makes a great lunch, dinner or appetizer. The melted feta is so delicious on the prosciutto.

Tip

This sandwich is also great served on sliced Italian bread.

- Panini grill or large skillet
- Preheat panini grill to medium, if using

8	slices whole-grain bread (½-inch/1 cm thick slices)	8
2 tbsp	olive oil	30 mL
¼ cup	Homemade Mayonnaise (page 188) or store-bought	60 mL
8 oz	thinly sliced prosciutto	250 g
1 cup	baby spinach leaves	250 mL
2	tomatoes, thinly sliced	2
4 oz	crumbled feta cheese	125 g

1. Brush one side of each bread slice with olive oil. Place on a work surface, oiled side down. Spread 4 bread slices equally with mayonnaise. Top equally with prosciutto, spinach, tomatoes and cheese. Cover with remaining bread slices, oiled side up, and press together gently.

2. Place sandwiches on preheated panini grill or in a large skillet over medium heat and cook, turning once if using a skillet, for 3 to 4 minutes or until golden brown and cheese is melted. Serve immediately.

Grilled Cheese Pizza Sandwich

Serves 4

Using marinara and pesto sauces creates awesome flavors in this sandwich. Serve with a tossed salad for lunch or dinner on busy weeknights.

- Panini grill or large skillet
- Preheat panini grill to medium, if using

8	slices Italian bread ($\frac{1}{2}$-inch/1 cm thick slices)	8
2 tbsp	olive oil	30 mL
$\frac{1}{4}$ cup	Basil Pesto (page 181) or store-bought	60 mL
$\frac{1}{4}$ cup	marinara sauce	60 mL
6 oz	sliced pepperoni	175 g
4	slices mozzarella cheese	4

1. Brush one side of each bread slice with olive oil. Place on a work surface, oiled side down. Spread 4 bread slices equally with pesto and the 4 other bottom halves with 1 tbsp (15 mL) of the marinara. Top marinara with pepperoni and cheese. Cover with remaining bread slices, oiled side up, and press together gently.

2. Place sandwiches on preheated panini grill or in a skillet over medium heat and cook, turning once if using a skillet, for 3 to 4 minutes or until golden brown and cheese is melted. Serve immediately.

Muffuletta Grilled Cheese

Serves 4

I love taking this New Orleans sandwich to a new level by cooking it as a grilled cheese. It doesn't get much better than this.

- Panini grill or large nonstick skillet
- Preheat panini grill to medium, if using

1/3 cup	chopped green olives	75 mL
1/3 cup	chopped black olives	75 mL
1	clove garlic, minced	1
2 tbsp	chopped fresh parsley	30 mL
1 tbsp	olive oil	15 mL
1/2 cup	olive juice	125 mL
1 tbsp	red wine vinegar	15 mL
8	slices French bread (1/2-inch/1 cm thick slices)	8
2 tbsp	olive oil	30 mL
8 oz	thinly sliced deli ham	250 g
8 oz	thinly sliced salami	250 g
4	slices provolone cheese	4

1. In a medium bowl, combine green olives, black olives, garlic, parsley, olive oil, olive juice and vinegar.

2. Brush one side of each bread slice with oil. Place on a work surface, oiled side down. Spread olive mixture equally over 4 bread slices. Top with ham and salami. Place 1 cheese slice on top and cover with remaining bread slice. Press together gently.

3. Place sandwiches in preheated panini grill or large nonstick skillet, turning once if using a skillet, for 3 to 5 minutes per side or until lightly browned and cheese is melted. Serve immediately.

Italian Salami Panini

Serves 4

*My 13-year old
daughter came up
with this panini
combination. I was
more than impressed
when I took a bite.*

Tip

I like the smaller circular
Italian salami slices.
Look for them in the
grocery store deli.

- **Panini grill or large skillet**
- **Preheat panini grill to medium, if using**

4	6-inch (15 cm) French bread loaves, cut in half lengthwise	4
¼ cup	butter or margarine, softened	60 mL
¼ cup	Homemade Mayonnaise (page 188) or store-bought	60 mL
8 oz	thin slices Italian salami (see Tip, left)	250 g
1 cup	mixed greens	250 mL
4	slices mozzarella cheese	4

1. Brush one side of each bread slice with butter. Place on a work surface, buttered side down. Spread mayonnaise equally over 4 of the bread slices. Top equally with salami, mixed greens and cheese. Cover with remaining bread slices, buttered side up, and press together gently.

2. Place sandwiches on preheated panini grill or in a large skillet over medium heat and cook, turning once if using a skillet, for 3 to 4 minutes or until golden brown and cheese is melted. Serve immediately.

Chorizo Melts

Chorizo is a ground pork sausage flavored with garlic and chili powder with a Spanish influence. It is so flavorful in this spicy warm sandwich.

- **Panini grill or large skillet**
- **Preheat panini grill to medium, if using**

12 oz	dry-cured chorizo, removed from casings and thinly sliced	375 g
8	slices sourdough bread (½-inch/1 cm thick slices)	8
¼ cup	butter or margarine, softened	60 mL
¼ cup	Homemade Mayonnaise (page 188) or store-bought	60 mL
4	slices pepper Jack cheese	4
2	tomatoes, thinly sliced	2

1. In a large skillet, cook chorizo over medium-high heat for 5 to 7 minutes or until lightly browned. Set aside.

2. Brush one side of each bread slice with butter. Place on a work surface, buttered side down. Spread 4 bread slices equally with mayonnaise. Top equally with chorizo, cheese and tomatoes. Cover with remaining bread slices, buttered side up, and press together gently.

3. Place sandwiches on preheated panini grill or in a large skillet over medium heat and cook, turning once if using a skillet, for 3 to 4 minutes or until golden brown and cheese is melted. Serve immediately.

Variations

If you can't find chorizo, you can use your favorite sausage.

Monterey Jack cheese may be used instead of pepper Jack.

Grilled Knockwurst and Swiss

Serves 4

Knockwurst, also called "knackwust," is a German-style hot dog that is great served with the Swiss cheese in this sandwich.

Tip

To grill knockwurst: Grill on a lightly greased grill over medium-high heat for 5 to 7 minutes.

- **Panini grill or large skillet**
- **Preheat panini grill to medium, if using**

8	slices rye bread ($\frac{1}{2}$-inch/1 cm thick slices)	8
$\frac{1}{4}$ cup	butter or margarine, softened	60 mL
$\frac{1}{4}$ cup	prepared mustard	60 mL
4	knockwurst, grilled and sliced lengthwise (see Tip, left)	4
4	slices Swiss cheese	4

1. Brush one side of each bread slice with butter. Place on a work surface, buttered side down. Spread 4 bread slices equally with mustard. Top equally with knockwurst slices and cheese. Cover with remaining bread slices, buttered side up, and press together gently.

2. Place sandwiches on preheated panini grill or in a large skillet over medium heat and cook, turning once if using a skillet, for 3 to 4 minutes or until golden brown and cheese is melted. Serve immediately.

Grilled Cowboy-Spiced Pork

This western-spiced pork is wonderful with pepper Jack cheese and avocado. I serve this with chips and salsa to start, and that's all you need.

- Preheat greased barbecue grill to medium-high
- Instant-read thermometer
- Panini grill or large skillet
- Preheat panini grill to medium, if using

3	cloves garlic, minced	3
2 tbsp	ground cumin	30 mL
1 tbsp	chili powder	15 mL
1/2 tsp	kosher salt	2 mL
1/4 tsp	hot pepper flakes	1 mL
4	boneless pork chops (about 1 1/2 lbs/750 g total)	4
1/4 cup	olive oil, divided	60 mL
2 tbsp	freshly squeezed lime juice	30 mL
8	slices crusty French bread (1/2-inch/1 cm thick slices)	8
1	avocado, thinly sliced	1
4	slices pepper Jack cheese	4

Toppings, optional

Salsa

Sour cream

1. In a small bowl, stir together garlic, cumin, chili powder, salt and hot pepper flakes. Rub over both sides of pork. Drizzle pork with 2 tbsp (30 mL) of the olive oil and lime juice.

2. Grill pork, turning once, for 10 to 12 minutes or until a meat thermometer inserted in thickest portion registers 155°F (68°C). Thinly slice pork.

3. Brush one side of each bread slice with remaining olive oil. Place on a work surface, oiled side down. Top 4 bread slices equally with pork, avocado, cheese and desired toppings. Cover with remaining bread slices, oiled side up, and press together gently.

4. Place sandwiches on preheated panini grill or a large skillet over medium heat and cook, turning once if using a skillet, for 3 to 4 minutes or until golden brown and cheese is melted. Serve immediately.

Variation

Monterey Jack cheese or a shredded Mexican cheese blend also works great in this sandwich instead of the pepper Jack.

Fish and Seafood

Smoked Salmon Pesto Grilled Cheese

Serves 4

This grilled cheese is perfect served with a summer tomato soup or a chopped vegetable salad.

Tip

Do not store tomatoes in the refrigerator as cool temperatures reduce their flavor. Store at room temperature. Once ripened, use within a few days.

- **Panini grill or large skillet**
- **Preheat panini grill to medium, if using**

8	slices Italian or multigrain bread (½-inch/1 cm thick slices)	8
¼ cup	butter or margarine, softened	60 mL
¼ cup	Basil Pesto (page 181) or store-bought	60 mL
12 oz	smoked salmon, thinly sliced	375 g
2	tomatoes, thinly sliced (see Tip, left)	2
4	slices mozzarella cheese	4

1. Brush one side of each bread slice with butter. Place on a work surface, buttered side down. Spread 4 bread slices equally Basil Pesto. Top equally with smoked salmon, sliced tomatoes and cheese. Cover with remaining bread slices, buttered side up, and press together gently.

2. Place sandwiches on preheated panini grill or in a large skillet over medium heat and cook, turning once if using a skillet, for 3 to 4 minutes or until golden brown and cheese is melted. Serve immediately.

Grilled Salmon and Gruyère

Gruyère cheese is my all-time favorite. It is great paired with the salmon in this grilled cheese.

- Panini grill or large skillet
- Preheat panini grill to medium-high, if using

8	slices sourdough bread (½-inch/1 cm thick slices)	8
2 tbsp	butter or margarine, softened	30 mL
8 oz	smoked salmon, thinly sliced	250 g
4 oz	Gruyère or Swiss cheese, thinly sliced	125 g
2	tomatoes, thinly sliced	2
½ cup	chopped fresh basil	125 mL

1. Brush one side of each bread slice with butter. Place on a work surface, buttered side down. Top 4 bread slices equally with smoked salmon, cheese, tomatoes and basil. Cover with remaining bread slices, buttered side up, and press together gently.

2. Place sandwiches on preheated panini grill or in a large skillet over medium-high heat and cook, turning once if using a skillet, for 3 to 4 minutes or until golden brown and cheese is melted. Serve immediately.

Grilled Salmon and Gorgonzola

This is an awesome grilled cheese sandwich that I love to make when I buy fresh salmon. It makes great use of Gorgonzola cheese.

Tip

Buy wild or Alaskan salmon when possible. I cook mine with the skin on because it holds the fish together and makes it easier to transfer from the grill.

- 11- by 7-inch (28 by 18 cm) glass baking dish, lined with foil
- Panini grill or large skillet
- Preheat oven to 400°F (200°C)
- Preheat panini grill to medium, if using

1¼ lbs	salmon fillets, skin on (see Tip, left)	625 g
½ tsp	sea salt	2 mL
½ tsp	paprika	2 mL
¼ tsp	cayenne pepper	1 mL
2 tbsp	freshly squeezed lemon juice	30 mL
3 tbsp	olive oil, divided	45 mL
8	slices sourdough bread (½-inch/1 cm thick slices)	8
1 cup	arugula leaves	250 mL
4 oz	crumbled Gorgonzola cheese	125 g

1. Place salmon, skin side down, in prepared baking dish. Season with salt, paprika and cayenne. Drizzle with lemon juice and 1 tbsp (15 mL) of the olive oil. Bake in preheated oven for 10 minutes or until salmon flakes easily when tested with a fork. Slice into 4 pieces.

2. Brush one side of each bread slice with remaining olive oil. Place on a work surface, oiled side down. Top 4 bread slices equally with salmon, arugula and cheese. Cover with remaining bread slices, oiled side up, and press together gently.

3. Place sandwiches on preheated panini grill or in a large skillet over medium heat and cook, turning once if using a skillet, for 3 to 4 minutes or until golden brown and cheese is melted. Serve immediately.

Grilled Turkey Cobb (page 126)

Grilled Ham, Goat Cheese and Figs (page 134)

Black Russian (page 137)

Grilled Salmon and Gruyère (page 159)

Grilled Crab, Mango and Avocado (page 173)

Basil Pesto (page 181)

Hummus (page 185)

Brie and Raspberry Panini with Hazelnut Spread (page 206)

Grilled Balsamic, Strawberry and Mascarpone Sandwich (page 207)

Spicy Paprika Salmon–Goat Cheese Sandwich

Serves 4

Chipotle seasoning can be found in the spice aisle of the grocery store. If you prefer less spicy food, use only 1 to 2 tsp (5 to 10 mL) chipotle seasoning.

Tip

For best results and optimal freshness, try to cook salmon within 24 hours of its purchase.

- **Preheat greased barbecue grill to medium-high**
- **Panini grill or large skillet**
- **Preheat panini grill to medium, if using**

2 tbsp	paprika	30 mL
1 tbsp	chipotle seasoning	15 mL
2	clove garlic, minced	2
1/2 tsp	kosher salt	2 mL
1 1/2 lbs	salmon fillets (see Tip, left)	750 g
1/3 cup	freshly squeezed lemon juice	75 mL
4 tbsp	olive oil, divided	60 mL
8	slices Italian bread (1/2-inch/ 1 cm thick slices)	8
1/2 cup	Homemade Mayonnaise (page 188) or store-bought	125 mL
1/2 cup	arugula	125 mL
1 cup	crumbled goat cheese	250 mL

1. In a small bowl, combine paprika, chipotle seasoning, garlic and salt. Rub over salmon. Drizzle salmon with lemon juice and 2 tbsp (30 mL) of the olive oil.

2. Place salmon on a lightly greased grill rack or grill pan coated with cooking spray. Grill over medium-high heat for 5 minutes or until fish flakes easily when pierced with a fork. Cut salmon into 4 pieces.

3. Brush one side of each bread slice with remaining 2 tbsp (30 mL) of olive oil. Place on a work surface, oiled side down. Spread mayonnaise equally over bottom halves. Top equally with salmon, arugula and cheese. Cover with top halves, oiled side up, and press together gently.

4. Place sandwiches on preheated panini grill or in a large skillet over medium heat and cook, turning once if using a skillet, for 3 to 4 minutes or until golden brown and cheese is melted. Serve immediately.

Grilled Flounder and Feta Cheese

Serves 4

I cook a lot of flounder at my house, and this recipe was a result of some leftovers. It came out great with melted feta.

Tips

There are concerns about the sustainability of some fish and seafood so we recommend you check reliable sites such as www.seachoice.org for the latest information.

Let lemons come to room temperature before juicing for more juice.

Feta is a white Greek cheese that has a tangy flavor. It's made from goat's milk, sheep's milk or a combination. I use low-fat feta. You can find it crumbled in the cheese section at the grocery store.

• **Preheat lightly greased barbecue grill to medium heat**

1½ lbs	flounder fillets	750 g
½ tsp	sea salt	2 mL
½ tsp	freshly ground black pepper	2 mL
½ tsp	paprika	2 mL
¼ cup	freshly squeezed lemon juice (see Tips, left)	60 mL
8	slices Italian bread (½-inch/1 cm thick slices)	8
2 tbsp	butter or margarine, softened	30 mL
¼ cup	Tartar Sauce (page 191) or store-bought	60 mL
1 cup	baby spinach leaves	250 mL
4 oz	crumbled feta cheese (see Tips, left)	125 g

1. Season flounder with salt, pepper and paprika. Drizzle with lemon juice. Grill for 6 minutes or until fish flakes easily with a fork. Slice into 4 pieces and then set aside. Leave barbecue grill on.

2. Brush one side of each bread slice with butter. Place on a work surface, buttered side down. Spread 4 bread slices equally with tartar sauce. Top equally with flounder, spinach and cheese. Cover with remaining bread slices, buttered side up, and press together gently.

3. Place sandwiches on preheated barbecue grill. Cook, turning once, for 3 to 4 minutes or until golden brown and cheese is melted. Serve immediately.

Variation

Substitute any white fish fillets, such as halibut or tilapia, for the flounder.

Hot Tuna Melts

Serves 4

Hot Tuna Melts are ideal for an easy weekend lunch or quick weeknight dinner. Serve with a salad or bowl of soup, and you've got your meal ready to go.

- Panini grill or large skillet
- Preheat panini grill to medium, if using

8	slices sourdough bread (½-inch/1 cm thick slices)	8
2 tbsp	olive oil	30 mL
2	cans (each 6 oz/170 g) solid white tuna, packed in water, drained	2
⅓ cup	Homemade Mayonnaise (page 188) or store-bought	75 mL
½ tsp	grated lemon zest	2 mL
1 tbsp	freshly squeezed lemon juice	15 mL
½ cup	finely chopped celery	125 mL
1 tbsp	finely chopped sweet pickles	15 mL
¼ tsp	freshly ground black pepper	1 mL
4	Kaiser rolls, split	4
4 oz	shredded white Cheddar cheese	125 g

1. Brush one side of each bread slice with olive oil. Place bread on a work surface, oiled side down.

2. In a large bowl, combine tuna, mayonnaise, lemon zest, lemon juice, celery, pickles and pepper.

3. Place bread slices on a work surface. Spread tuna mixture equally over 4 bread slices and add cheese. Cover with remaining bread slices, oiled side up, and press together gently.

4. Place sandwiches on preheated panini grill or in a large skillet over medium heat, and cook, turning once if using a skillet, for 3 to 4 minutes or until golden brown and cheese is melted. Serve immediately.

Variation

Substitute Swiss or Gruyère cheese for the Cheddar cheese in this recipe.

Grilled Grouper with Red Peppers and Feta

This seafood grilled cheese is complemented by the colorful red pepper, mint and feta topping.

Tip

Prepare the red pepper topping up to 2 days ahead of time to make preparation even quicker and easier.

- **Panini grill or large skillet**
- **Preheat panini grill to medium, if using**

1/2 cup	finely chopped red bell pepper	125 mL
2 tbsp	finely chopped red onion	30 mL
4 tbsp	finely chopped fresh mint, divided	60 mL
6 tbsp	freshly squeezed lemon juice, divided	90 mL
1 tsp	Dijon mustard	5 mL
3 tbsp	olive oil, divided	45 mL
1 cup	crumbled feta cheese	250 mL
1 1/2 lbs	grouper or cod fillets, cut into 4 equal pieces	750 g
1/2 tsp	sea salt	2 mL
1/2 tsp	freshly ground black pepper	2 mL
8	Italian bread slices (1/2-inch/1 cm thick slices)	8
2 tbsp	butter, softened	30 mL

1. In a bowl, stir together bell pepper, red onion, 2 tbsp (30 mL) of the chopped mint, 3 tbsp (45 mL) of the lemon juice, Dijon mustard, 1 tbsp (15 mL) of the oil and feta. Set aside.

2. Season both sides of fish with remaining chopped mint, salt and pepper. Drizzle with remaining lemon juice.

3. In a large nonstick skillet, heat remaining 2 tbsp (30 mL) of olive oil over medium heat. Add fish and cook for 4 to 6 minutes on each side or until desired degree of doneness. Remove from skillet and wipe clean.

4. Brush one side of each bread slice with butter. Place on a work surface, buttered side down. Top equally with fish and red pepper topping. Cover with remaining bread slices, buttered side up, and press together gently.

5. Place sandwiches on a preheated panini grill or in a large skillet over medium heat and cook, turning once if using a skillet, for 3 to 4 minutes or until golden brown and cheese is melted. Serve immediately.

~~~~~~~~~~~~~~~~~~~~~~~~~~~~~~~~

Variation

Serve on 4 Kaiser buns instead of Italian bread.

Grilled Tilapia, Goat Cheese and Avocado

Goat cheese and avocado provide wonderful texture and flavors in this fabulous grilled cheese recipe.

Tip

There are concerns about the sustainability of some fish and seafood so we recommend you check reliable sites such as www.seachoice.org for the latest information.

1 tbsp	balsamic vinegar	15 mL
1 tsp	liquid honey	5 mL
1 tsp	freshly squeezed lime juice	5 mL
1 tsp	Dijon mustard	5 mL
1 lb	tilapia fillets, cut into 4 pieces	500 g
2	avocados, chopped	2
1 cup	chopped pineapple	250 mL
½ cup	chopped red onion	125 mL
¼ cup	chopped red bell pepper	60 mL
2 tbsp	chopped fresh cilantro	30 mL
1 tbsp	sesame oil	15 mL
4	sandwich buns, split and toasted	4
2 tbsp	butter, softened	30 mL
4 oz	crumbled goat cheese	125 g

1. In a small bowl, combine balsamic vinegar, honey, lime juice and Dijon mustard. Place fish fillets in a large shallow dish and drizzle with balsamic marinade. Let stand for 10 minutes.

2. In another small bowl, combine avocados, pineapple, red onion, bell pepper and cilantro until chunky.

3. In a large skillet, heat oil over medium heat. Add fish and cook for 4 minutes on each side or until fish flakes easily with a fork. Remove fish from skillet and wipe skillet clean.

4. Brush one side of buns with butter. Place on a work surface, buttered side down. Top 4 halves equally with fish, avocado mixture and goat cheese. Cover with remaining bun half, buttered side up, and press together gently.

5. Place sandwiches in skillet over medium heat and cook, turning once, for 3 to 4 minutes or until golden brown and cheese is melted. Serve immediately.

Variation

Substitute any white fish fillets, such as flounder, snapper or Pacific halibut for the tilapia.

Shrimp Gremolata Panini

Gremolata is a mixture of parsley, lemon and garlic. It pairs well with the shrimp and provolone in this flavorful grilled cheese.

Tip

Once lemon zest is removed from a lemon, the lemon can be refrigerated for up to 1 week.

- **Panini grill or large skillet**
- **Preheat panini grill to medium, if using**

1 lb	cooked shrimp (see Tip, page 169)	500 g
2	cloves garlic, minced	2
3 tbsp	chopped fresh Italian flat-leaf parsley	45 mL
1 tsp	grated lemon zest	5 mL
8	slices French bread (1/2-inch/1 cm thick slices)	8
2 tbsp	olive oil	30 mL
4	slices provolone cheese	4

1. In a large bowl, toss together shrimp, garlic, parsley and lemon zest.

2. Brush one side of each bread slice with olive oil. Place on a work surface, oiled side down. Top 4 bread slices equally with shrimp mixture and cheese. Cover with remaining bread slices, oiled side up, and press together gently.

3. Place sandwiches on preheated panini grill or in a large skillet over medium heat and cook, turning once if using a skillet, for 3 to 4 minutes or until golden brown and cheese is melted. Serve immediately.

Grilled Shrimp Parmesan

Serves 4

This Italian-style shrimp sandwich is great to serve for lunch and dinner. It's my family's favorite spring and summertime sandwich.

Tip

Fresh shrimp cook very quickly. In a skillet, heat 1 tbsp (15 mL) olive oil over medium heat. Cook shrimp, stirring frequently, for about 2 minutes per side or until pink and opaque. Pour in a colander to drain.

- **Panini grill or large skillet**
- **Preheat panini grill to medium, if using**

8	slices Italian bread (½-inch/1 cm thick slices)	8
¼ cup	olive oil	60 mL
1 lb	cooked shrimp (see Tip, left)	500 g
¾ cup	fresh basil leaves	175 mL
½ cup	freshly grated Parmesan cheese	125 mL

1. Brush one side of each bread slice with olive oil. Place on a work surface, oiled side down. Top 4 bread slices equally with shrimp, basil and cheese. Cover with remaining bread slices, oiled side up, and press together gently.

2. Place sandwiches on preheated panini grill or in a large skillet over medium heat and cook, turning once if using a skillet, for 3 to 4 minutes or until golden brown and cheese is melted. Serve immediately.

Variation

Sourdough bread can be substituted for the Italian.

Shrimp, Mushroom and Fontina

I love shrimp, mushrooms and fontina, so this grilled cheese is heaven to me. We serve these a lot for simple entertaining, and guests love them.

- **Panini grill or large skillet**
- **Preheat panini grill to medium, if using**

8	slices Italian bread ($\frac{1}{2}$-inch/1 cm thick slices)	8
2 tbsp	butter or margarine, softened	30 mL
1 lb	cooked shrimp (see Tip, page 169)	500 g
1$\frac{1}{3}$ cups	sliced fresh button mushrooms	325 mL
$\frac{1}{2}$ cup	grated fontina cheese	125 mL

1. Brush one side of each bread slice with butter. Place on a work surface, buttered side down. Top 4 bread slices equally with shrimp, mushrooms and cheese. Cover with remaining bread slices, buttered side up, and press together gently.

2. Place sandwiches on preheated panini grill or in a large skillet over medium heat and cook, turning once if using a skillet, for 3 to 4 minutes or until golden brown and cheese is melted. Serve immediately.

Shrimp-Avocado Grilled Cheese

Shrimp, avocado and Havarti are three of my favorite ingredients that work well together in this mouthwatering sandwich.

- Panini grill or large skillet
- Preheat panini grill to medium, if using

8	slices Italian bread (½-inch/1 cm thick slices)	8
2 tbsp	olive oil	30 mL
1 lb	cooked shrimp (see Tip, page 169)	500 g
2	tomatoes, thinly sliced	2
2	avocados, thinly sliced	2
4	thin slices Havarti cheese	4

1. Brush one side of each bread slice with olive oil. Place on a work surface, oiled side down. Top 4 bread slices equally with shrimp, tomatoes, avocados and cheese. Cover with remaining bread slices, oiled side up, and press together gently.

2. Place sandwiches on preheated panini grill or in a large skillet over medium heat and cook, turning once if using a skillet, for 3 to 4 minutes or until golden brown and cheese is melted. Serve immediately.

Crab Mushroom Melts

These sandwiches are delightful served with a side of slaw or a spinach salad.

Tip

When purchasing crab, I figure 3 to 4 oz (90 to 125 g) per person.

- **Preheat broiler**
- **Panini grill or large skillet**
- **Preheat panini grill to medium, if using**

¼ cup + 2 tbsp	butter or margarine, softened, divided	90 mL
1½ cups	sliced fresh mushrooms	375 mL
2 tbsp	Homemade Mayonnaise (page 188) or store-bought	30 mL
1 tbsp	Dijon mustard	15 mL
1 tbsp	white wine vinegar	15 mL
½ tsp	dried oregano	2 mL
⅛ tsp	freshly ground black pepper	0.5 mL
2 cups	crabmeat, shell pieces removed (about 12 oz/375 g) (see Tip, left)	500 mL
8	slices sourdough bread (½-inch/1 cm slices)	8
4 oz	Muenster cheese, cut into 4 slices	125 g

1. In a large nonstick skillet, melt 2 tbsp (30 mL) of the butter over medium heat. Add mushrooms and cook, stirring frequently, for 4 minutes or until tender. Drain and set aside.

2. In a medium bowl, combine mayonnaise, mustard, vinegar, oregano and pepper. Add crabmeat and mushrooms and toss gently to coat.

3. Brush one side of each bread slice with remaining butter. Place on a work surface, buttered side down. Spoon crabmeat mixture on 4 bread slices. Top with cheese and press bread slices together, buttered side up.

4. Place sandwiches on preheated panini grill or in a large skillet over medium heat and cook, turning once if using a skillet, for 3 to 4 minutes or until golden brown and cheese is melted. Serve immediately.

Grilled Crab, Mango and Avocado

This sandwich is wonderful for summer entertaining at home, the lake or at the beach.

Tips

Avocados turn brown quickly but brushing with lemon juice will help it some. If you end up with half of a cut avocado, store it with the pit still in it and wrapped tightly in plastic in the refrigerator.

If you're short on time, purchase jarred mango slices and use 1 cup (250 mL), drained.

- Panini grill or large skillet
- Preheat panini grill to medium, if using

12 oz	fresh crabmeat, drained	375 g
3 tbsp	freshly squeezed lime juice	45 mL
1/8 tsp	freshly ground black pepper	0.5 mL
8	slices French bread (1/2-inch/1 cm thick slices)	8
1/4 cup	butter or margarine, softened	60 mL
2	avocados, sliced (see Tips, left)	2
1	mango, thinly sliced (see Tips, left)	1
4 oz	Muenster cheese, thinly sliced	125 g

1. In a medium bowl, combine crab, lime juice and pepper.

2. Brush one side of each bread slice with butter. Place on a work surface, buttered side down. Top 4 bread slices equally with crab mixture, avocados, mango and cheese. Cover with remaining bread slices, buttered side up, and press together gently.

3. Place sandwiches on preheated panini grill or in a large skillet over medium heat and cook, turning once if using a skillet, for 3 to 4 minutes or until golden brown and cheese is melted. Serve immediately.

Variation

Omit mango and use 1 cup (250 mL) Nectarine Salsa (Variation, page 179) or Peach Salsa (page 179) instead.

Condiments

Peach-Ginger Chutney

Makes 2½ cups (625 mL)		

This chutney is delicious served on top of cold sandwiches and hot sandwiches, including burgers.

2	peaches, chopped (about 2 cups/500 mL)	2
3 tbsp	peach preserves or jam	45 mL
2 tbsp	rice wine vinegar	30 mL
1 tbsp	grated fresh gingerroot	15 mL
¼ tsp	kosher salt	1 mL
2 tbsp	chopped green onions	30 mL

1. In a small saucepan over medium heat, simmer peaches, preserves, rice wine vinegar, ginger and salt, stirring occasionally, for 10 to 15 minutes or until liquid has evaporated. Stir in green onions. Use immediately or cover and refrigerate for up to 3 days.

Variation

Plum Chutney: Substitute 2 cups (500 mL) plums for the peaches and omit the ginger.

Mango Chutney

Makes 2½ cups (625 mL)		

This chutney is delicious served on top of hot and cold sandwiches.

2 cups	chopped mango	500 mL
3 tbsp	mango preserves or jam	45 mL
2 tbsp	rice wine vinegar	30 mL
1 tbsp	grated fresh gingerroot	15 mL
¼ tsp	kosher salt	1 mL
2 tbsp	chopped green onions	30 mL

1. In a small saucepan over medium heat, simmer mangos, preserves, rice wine vinegar, ginger and salt, stirring occasionally, for 10 to 15 minutes or until liquid has evaporated. Stir in green onions. Use immediately or cover and refrigerate for up to 3 days.

Variation

You can substitute 3 tbsp (45 mL) peach preserves or jam for the mango.

Sweet Pepper Relish

**Makes
2½ cups
(625 mL)**

This relish is great on crostini, bagel chips, crackers, turkey, beef, fish or poultry.

Tip

You could also roast the peppers in a preheated 500°F (260°C) oven for 10 minutes or until tender.

- **Preheat oven to 400°F (200°C)**
- **Large baking dish, coated with cooking spray**

1	red bell pepper, diced	1
1	yellow bell pepper, diced	1
1	small onion, diced	1
2	cloves garlic, minced	2
1 tbsp	olive oil	15 mL
1 tbsp	balsamic vinegar	15 mL
½ tsp	sea salt	2 mL
½ tsp	dried Italian seasoning	2 mL

1. In a medium bowl, stir together red and yellow bell peppers, onion, garlic, olive oil, vinegar, salt and Italian seasoning. Transfer to prepared baking dish. Bake in preheated oven for 45 minutes or until vegetables are softened.

2. Transfer to a bowl and let cool for at least 30 minutes. Use immediately or cover and refrigerate for up to 2 days.

Cherry Tomato Relish

*This relish is perfect
for any summertime
sandwich. It is also
wonderful on top
of Brie, crackers
or crostini.*

Tip

I like to store fresh
tomatoes at room
temperature away from
direct sunlight. Cold
temperatures destroy
the fresh flavors of
the tomatoes.

2½ cups	halved cherry tomatoes (see Tip, left)	625 mL
¼ cup	sliced black olives	60 mL
2	green onions, chopped	2
2 tbsp	balsamic vinegar	30 mL
1 tbsp	extra virgin olive oil	15 mL
2 tsp	chopped fresh oregano	10 mL
¼ tsp	salt	1 mL
¼ tsp	freshly ground black pepper	1 mL

1. In a small bowl, combine cherry tomatoes, olives, green onions, vinegar, oil, oregano, salt and pepper. Use immediately or cover and refrigerate for up to 2 days.

Peach Salsa

This summery salsa is best with ripe peaches. It complements fish, chicken, beef or pork dishes, especially when they're grilled.

2	ripe peaches, peeled and diced	2
1	medium red bell pepper, diced	1
1	jalapeño pepper, seeded and diced	1
½	red onion, chopped	½
¼ cup	chopped fresh cilantro	60 mL
2 tbsp	chopped fresh mint	30 mL
2 tbsp	freshly squeezed lime juice	30 mL
1 tbsp	liquid honey	15 mL
¼ tsp	cayenne pepper	1 mL
¼ tsp	salt	1 mL

1. In a medium bowl, combine peaches, bell pepper, jalapeño, red onion, cilantro, mint, lime juice, honey, cayenne and salt. Cover and refrigerate for at least 30 minutes or for up to 3 days.

Variation

Nectarine Salsa: Substitute 2 nectarines for the peaches.

Pico de Gallo

I love this salsa-type of spread. It's great on any Southwestern sandwich, taco or fajita, or served with tortilla chips.

4	large tomatoes, peeled, seeded and chopped	4
⅓ cup	diced red onion	75 mL
1 tsp	jalapeño pepper, seeded and diced	5 mL
½ cup	chopped fresh cilantro	125 mL
2 tbsp	freshly squeezed lime juice	30 mL
½ tsp	ground cumin	2 mL
¼ tsp	chili powder	1 mL

1. In a medium bowl, combine tomatoes, red onion, jalapeño, cilantro, lime juice, cumin and chili powder. Cover and refrigerate until ready to use or for up to 2 days.

Guacamole

This guacamole is wonderful on any sandwich or also perfect for an appetizer with tortilla chips.

Tip

I prefer using Hass avocados. When selecting avocados, look for ones that are heavy for their size and unblemished. Store unripe avocados at room temperature, and once they are ripe, in the refrigerator for up to 5 days.

4	ripe Hass avocados, diced (see Tip, right)	4
½ cup	diced red onion (1 small onion)	125 mL
1	large clove garlic, minced	1
3 tbsp	freshly squeezed lemon juice (1 lemon)	45 mL
½ tsp	hot pepper sauce	2 mL
1	medium tomato, seeded and diced	1
1 tsp	freshly ground black pepper	5 mL
½ tsp	kosher salt	2 mL

1. In a medium bowl, combine avocados, red onion, garlic, lemon juice and hot pepper sauce. Gently stir in tomato, pepper and salt. Use immediately or cover and refrigerate for up to 2 days.

Basil Pesto

*Fresh Basil Pesto makes
any sandwich taste
better. I love it on
vegetarian sandwiches
because it gives them
such a depth of flavor.*

Tip

I prefer extra virgin olive
oil, derived from the first
pressing of the olives,
because it has the most
delicate flavor and the
most antioxidant benefits.

• **Food processor or blender**

½ cup	packed fresh basil leaves	125 mL
½ cup	freshly grated Parmesan cheese	125 mL
¼ cup	pine nuts, toasted (see Tips, page 187)	60 mL
¼ cup	walnuts, toasted (see Tip, page 22)	60 mL
⅔ cup	extra virgin olive oil (see Tip, left)	150 mL
2	cloves garlic, coarsely chopped	2
1 tbsp	freshly squeezed lemon juice	15 mL
½ tsp	salt	2 mL
½ tsp	freshly ground black pepper	2 mL

1. In a food processor or blender, process basil,
Parmesan, pine nuts, walnuts, oil, garlic, lemon juice,
salt and pepper until smooth, stopping once to scrape
down sides. Use immediately or cover and refrigerate
for up to 3 days.

Sun-Dried Tomato Pesto

**Makes
1½ cups
(375 mL)**

*This pesto is one
of my favorites. I
lather it on so many
sandwiches and also
serve it as an appetizer
with vegetables
and crackers.*

● **Food processor or blender**

2	cloves garlic, minced	2
½ cup	sun-dried tomatoes, undrained	125 mL
2 tbsp	chopped fresh basil	30 mL
⅛ tsp	salt	0.5 mL
⅛ tsp	freshly ground black pepper	0.5 mL
2 tbsp	freshly grated Parmesan cheese	30 mL

1. In a food processor or blender, process garlic, sun-dried tomatoes, basil, salt and pepper until smooth. Stir in cheese and process again until smooth. Use immediately or cover and refrigerate for up to 3 days.

Roasted Asparagus Pesto

**Makes
1¹⁄₂ cups
(375 mL)**

*This pesto is perfect
on any vegetarian
sandwich as well as
steak, chicken and
turkey sandwiches.*

- Preheat oven to 400°F (200°C)
- Large baking sheet, lined with parchment paper
- Food processor

1 lb	asparagus, cut into ¹⁄₂-inch (1 cm) pieces	500 g
¹⁄₄ cup + 2 tbsp	olive oil, divided	90 mL
2 tbsp	grated lemon zest	30 mL
	Kosher salt and freshly ground black pepper	
³⁄₄ cup	freshly grated Parmesan cheese	175 mL
¹⁄₄ cup	chopped pine nuts, toasted (see Tips, page 187)	60 mL
1	clove garlic, minced	1
2 tbsp	freshly squeezed lemon juice	30 mL

1. Place asparagus in a single layer on prepared baking sheet. Drizzle with 2 tbsp (30 mL) of the olive oil. Sprinkle with lemon zest, ¹⁄₂ tsp (2 mL) salt and ¹⁄₄ tsp (1 mL) pepper. Bake in preheated oven for 8 to 10 minutes or until tender. Let cool slightly.

2. In a food processor, process asparagus, cheese, pine nuts, garlic and lemon juice until combined. With processor running, slowly add remaining oil through the feed tube. Season with ¹⁄₄ tsp (1 mL) each salt and pepper. Use immediately or cover and refrigerate for up to 2 days.

Variation
Walnuts or almonds can be substituted for the pine nuts.

Cilantro Pesto

**Makes 2 cups
(500 mL)**

This pesto, made with cilantro, adds unique flavor to burgers, wraps and even on top of crostini.

Tip

I used Parmigiano-Reggiano Parmesan cheese, but if you can't find it or don't have it on hand, the regular version is fine.

● **Food processor or blender**

¹⁄₂ cup	loosely packed fresh cilantro leaves	125 mL
¹⁄₂ cup	freshly grated Parmesan cheese (see Tip, left)	125 mL
¹⁄₄ cup	pine nuts	60 mL
3	cloves garlic, coarsely chopped	3
2 tbsp	olive oil	30 mL
1 tbsp	freshly squeezed lime juice	15 mL
¹⁄₂ tsp	salt	2 mL
¹⁄₄ tsp	ground cumin	1 mL

1. In a food processor or blender, process cilantro, Parmesan, pine nuts, garlic, oil, lime juice, salt and cumin until smooth, stopping once to scrape down sides. Use immediately or cover and refrigerate for up to 3 days.

~~~~~~

Variation

Arugula Pesto: Substitute ¹⁄₂ cup (125 mL) arugula for the cilantro leaves.

Hummus

Makes about 3 cups (750 mL)

When I make homemade hummus, my family loves it. I try to lighten it up a bit by omitting the olive oil and adding the liquid from the chickpeas.

● **Food processor**

4	cloves garlic, coarsely chopped	4
2 cups	canned chickpeas, drained, liquid reserved	500 mL
6 tbsp	freshly squeezed lemon juice (about 2 lemons)	90 mL
1/3 cup	tahini (sesame paste)	75 mL
2 tbsp	water or liquid from the chickpeas	30 mL
1 1/2 tsp	kosher salt	7 mL
1 tsp	hot pepper sauce	5 mL

Toppings, optional

Cayenne pepper

Paprika

Olive oil

1. In a food processor, purée garlic, chickpeas, lemon juice, tahini, water or chickpea liquid, salt and hot pepper sauce. Top with desired toppings, if using.

Variation

Substitute 2 tbsp (30 mL) extra virgin olive oil for the reserved chickpea liquid if you want a stronger olive flavor.

Red Pepper Hummus

This hummus is a twist on regular hummus but gives all sandwiches a wonderful kick. It also works great as an appetizer served with pita triangles and crudités.

Tip

Tahini is a thick paste made of ground sesame seeds and is found in Middle Eastern cooking. Look for it in the international section of the grocery store.

● **Food processor**

1	can (14 to 19 oz/398 to 540 mL) chickpeas, drained and rinsed	1
⅓ cup	roasted red peppers from a jar, drained	75 mL
2	cloves garlic, coarsely chopped	2
¼ cup	tahini (see Tip, left)	60 mL
2 tbsp	minced Italian flat-leaf parsley	30 mL
2 tbsp	freshly squeezed lemon juice	30 mL
1½ tsp	ground cumin	7 mL
¼ tsp	kosher salt	1 mL
¼ tsp	cayenne pepper	1 mL

1. In a food processor, purée chickpeas, roasted peppers, garlic, tahini, parsley, lemon juice, cumin, salt and cayenne until smooth. Use immediately or cover and refrigerate for up to 2 days.

Variation

Cannellini or white beans may be substituted for chickpeas in this recipe. Be sure to drain and rinse beans before using.

Caponata Spread

This spread is wonderful on hamburgers, fish and chicken as well as perfect served as an appetizer.

Tips

Pine nuts, also called, pignoli, are the seeds from the cone of certain pine trees. They turn rancid quickly and should be refrigerated for no more than 1 month.

To toast pine nuts: Place pine nuts in a hot dry skillet over medium heat, stirring occasionally, for 4 minutes or until lightly browned. Or place nuts in a single layer on a baking sheet in a preheated 375°F (190°C) oven, stirring once or twice, for 5 minutes or until fragrant and golden.

Preheat oven to 450°F (230°C)

1	medium eggplant, thinly sliced	1
2 tbsp	olive oil	30 mL
1	clove garlic, minced	1
½ tsp	salt	2 mL
¼ tsp	freshly ground black pepper	1 mL
4	Roma (plum) tomatoes, thinly sliced	4
1	small red onion, thinly sliced	1
2 tbsp	chopped kalamata olives	30 mL
2 tbsp	drained capers, rinsed	30 mL
2 tbsp	pine nuts, toasted (see Tips, left)	30 mL
3 tbsp	red wine or balsamic vinegar	45 mL
1 tsp	liquid honey	5 mL
2 tbsp	chopped Italian flat-leaf parsley	30 mL

1. On a large baking sheet, place eggplant in a single layer. Drizzle with olive oil and season with garlic, salt and pepper. Bake in preheated oven for 15 minutes. Add tomatoes and red onion and bake for 15 minutes more. Let cool slightly.

2. In a large bowl, combine eggplant, tomatoes, red onion, olives, capers, pine nuts, vinegar, honey and parsley. Use immediately or cover and refrigerate for up to 2 days.

Homemade Mayonnaise

*If you ever want to
make homemade
mayonnaise, this
recipe is for you. It's
as easy as can be
and wonderful served
on anything.*

Tip

This recipe contains raw
eggs. If you are concerned
about the safety of using
raw eggs, use pasteurized
eggs in the shell or $\frac{1}{4}$ cup
(60 mL) pasteurized liquid
whole eggs.

• **Food processor or blender**

1	egg (see Tip, left)	1
1 tbsp	freshly squeezed lemon juice	15 mL
1 tsp	Dijon mustard	5 mL
$\frac{3}{4}$ cup	extra virgin olive oil	175 mL
	Salt and freshly ground black pepper	

1. In a food processor or blender, process egg, lemon
   juice and mustard until smooth. With motor running,
   add oil in a slow steady stream through the feed tube
   until mixture thickens and emulsifies. Season with
   salt and pepper to taste. Use immediately or cover and
   refrigerate for up to 2 days.

Fresh Basil Aïoli

*Serve basil aïoli on top
of any type of sandwich
or serve with vegetables
and crackers.*

Tips

Reduced-fat mayonnaise
can be substituted for
regular.

A key to success in making
aïoli is to add the oil
very slowly.

● **Food processor or blender**

1	clove garlic, coarsely chopped	1
1 cup	fresh basil leaves	250 mL
1 cup	Homemade Mayonnaise (page 188) or store-bought	250 mL
1 tbsp	Dijon mustard	15 mL
½ tsp	grated lemon zest	2 mL
½ tsp	freshly squeezed lemon juice	2 mL
¼ tsp	kosher salt	1 mL
1 tbsp	extra virgin olive oil	15 mL

1. In a food processor or blender, process garlic, basil, mayonnaise, mustard, lemon zest, lemon juice and salt until smooth. With processor running, slowly drizzle oil through the feed tube until slightly thickened. (This must be done very slowly or the oil will not emulsify and your sauce will not thicken.) Use immediately or cover and refrigerate for up to 3 days.

Chipotle Aïoli

This sauce is great on burgers, steak, pork or chicken. It has a kick but also a hint of fresh lime.

Tips

Reduced-fat mayonnaise may be substituted for regular.

You can find chipotle chile peppers in adobo sauce in a can in the international section of the grocery store.

½ cup	Homemade Mayonnaise (page 188) or store-bought	125 mL
2 tbsp	chopped chipotle chiles in adobo sauce (see Tips, left)	30 mL
1 tbsp	chopped fresh cilantro	15 mL
1 tsp	freshly grated lime zest	5 mL
1 tsp	freshly squeezed lime juice	5 mL

1. In a small bowl, combine mayonnaise, chipotle chiles, cilantro, lime zest and lime juice. Cover and refrigerate for up to 2 days.

Tartar Sauce

**Makes 1 cup
(250 mL)**

*This classic version
of tartar sauce is my
favorite. I love it on
top of any seafood
sandwich or as a
dipping sauce.*

Tip

Be careful when chopping
jalapeños. Make sure you
wash your hands well
before touching your eyes.

¾ cup	Homemade Mayonnaise (page 188) or store-bought	175 mL
¼ cup	freshly squeezed lime juice	60 mL
2 tbsp	chopped pickles	30 mL
2 tbsp	chopped red onion	30 mL
2 tbsp	chopped Italian flat-leaf parsley	30 mL
1 tsp	chopped jalapeño (see Tip, left)	5 mL

1. In a medium bowl, combine mayonnaise, lime juice, pickles, red onion, parsley and jalapeño. Cover and refrigerate until serving for up to 2 days.

Barbecue Sauce

This simple barbecue sauce is so easy and is wonderful anytime you want a hearty classic barbecue sandwich.

¾ cup	apple cider vinegar	175 mL
½ cup	ketchup	125 mL
⅓ cup	chili sauce	75 mL
2 tbsp	Worcestershire sauce	30 mL
1	clove garlic, minced	1
⅛ tsp	cayenne pepper	0.5 mL

1. In a medium saucepan over medium heat, combine cider vinegar, ketchup, chili sauce, Worcestershire sauce, garlic and cayenne. Bring to a boil. Reduce heat and simmer, stirring occasionally, for 30 minutes. Use immediately or cover and refrigerate for up to 3 days.

Pimiento Cheese

Makes
1½ cups
(375 mL)

This Southern condiment makes the perfect grilled cheese or snack with crackers.

Tip

Shred Cheddar cheese by hand or by using a food processor. If you're using hard cheese, let it come to room temperature before serving.

¼ cup	Homemade Mayonnaise (page 188) or store-bought	60 mL
2 tbsp	finely chopped red onion	30 mL
4 oz	diced pimientos, drained	125 g
⅛ tsp	cayenne pepper	0.5 mL
4 oz	shredded sharp (aged) Cheddar cheese (see Tip, left)	125 g
4 oz	shredded white Cheddar cheese	125 g

1. In a medium bowl, combine mayonnaise, red onion, pimientos and cayenne. Gently stir in sharp and white Cheddar cheeses. Use immediately or cover and refrigerate for up to 3 days.

Goat Cheese and Honey Spread

**Makes ⅔ cup
(150 mL)**

This spread is so easy to make and extremely versatile as a dessert, breakfast or appetizer condiment.

4 oz	goat cheese, softened	125 g
2 tbsp	liquid honey	30 mL

1. In a medium bowl, combine goat cheese and honey. Use immediately or cover and refrigerate for up to 2 days.

Variation

Stir in cinnamon, nutmeg or pumpkin pie spice to flavor the goat cheese.

Honey-Walnut Cream Cheese

Makes 1 cup (250 mL)

This is a wonderful spread on a bagel or grilled cheese such as in Chocolate Hazelnut–Stuffed French Toast (page 30).

1	package (8 oz/250 g) reduced-fat cream cheese, softened	1
½ cup	chopped walnuts	125 mL
2 tbsp	liquid honey	30 mL
4 tsp	light brown sugar	20 mL
1 tsp	ground cinnamon	5 mL

1. In a food processor, blender or mixing bowl, combine cream cheese, walnuts, honey, brown sugar and cinnamon. Use immediately or refrigerate for up to 3 days.

Variation

To make Hazelnut Cream Cheese, stir in 2 tbsp (30 mL) chocolate-hazelnut spread.

Pumpkin Spice Cream Cheese

Makes 1 cup (250 mL)

This cream cheese is perfect during fall. Serve it on toast, bagels or in any of your favorite recipes where you use cream cheese.

Tip

I used canned pumpkin, which can be found where the canned fruits are sold in the grocery store.

1	package (8 oz/250 g) reduced-fat cream cheese, softened	1
1/4 cup	pumpkin purée (not pie filling) (see Tip, left)	60 mL
2 tbsp	pure maple syrup	30 mL
1 tbsp	light brown sugar	15 mL
1 tsp	ground cinnamon	5 mL
1 tsp	pumpkin pie spice	5 mL
1/2 tsp	ground nutmeg	2 mL

1. In a food processor, blender or mixing bowl, combine cream cheese, pumpkin, maple syrup, brown sugar, cinnamon, pumpkin pie spice and nutmeg. Use immediately or refrigerate for up to 3 days.

Garlic-Herb Cream Cheese

**Makes 1 cup
(250 mL)**

*Fresh herbs, garlic
and green onions
create a wonderful
spread to serve on
crostini, bagels, and
on your favorite grilled
cheese recipes.*

- **Food processor or blender**

1	package (8 oz/250 g) reduced-fat cream cheese, softened	1
3	green onions, white parts and a bit of green, chopped	3
2 tbsp	chopped fresh basil	30 mL
2 tbsp	chopped fresh parsley	30 mL
1	clove garlic	1
1/8 tsp	sea salt	0.5 mL

1. In a food processor or blender, pulse cream cheese, green onions, basil, parsley, garlic and sea salt until combined. Refrigerate for at least 30 minutes until chilled. Use immediately or refrigerate for up to 3 days.

Desserts

Grilled Pear, Walnut and Goat Cheese

This fall-inspired recipe is so creamy, crunchy and tasty all in one. I like to cut these into small pieces for appetizers as well.

Tip

Purchase pears when they are firm and not hard. To ripen faster, place in a paper bag or in a covered bowl. Once ripe, pears can be kept in the refrigerator for up to 3 days.

- **Panini grill or large skillet**
- **Preheat panini grill to medium, if using**

8	slices multigrain bread ($\frac{1}{2}$-inch/1 cm thick slices)	8
2 tbsp	butter or margarine, softened	30 mL
$\frac{1}{2}$ cup	pear preserves or jam	125 mL
2	pears, thinly sliced (see Tip, left)	2
1 cup	chopped walnuts, toasted (see Tip, page 22)	250 mL
4 oz	crumbled goat cheese	125 g

1. Brush one side of each bread slice with butter. Place on a work surface, buttered side down. Spread 8 bread slices equally with pear preserves. Top 4 slices equally with pears, walnuts and goat cheese. Press slices together gently, buttered side up.

2. Place sandwiches on preheated panini grill or in a large skillet over medium heat and cook, turning once if using a skillet, for 3 to 4 minutes or until golden brown and cheese is melted. Serve immediately.

Mascarpone and Brie–Stuffed Raisin Bread

Serves 4

I love this simple combination of mascarpone and Brie with a mix of honey. It's a great dessert and also works well as a sweet appetizer.

Tip

When using Brie, let it come to room temperature before using. The rind of the Brie is edible, but feel free to trim it off if you wish.

- Panini grill or large skillet
- Preheat panini grill to medium heat, if using

¼ cup	mascarpone, at room temperature	60 mL
¼ cup	liquid honey	60 mL
8	slices raisin bread (½-inch/1 cm thick slices)	8
¼ cup	butter or margarine	60 mL
4 oz	Brie, thinly sliced (see Tip, left)	125 g

1. In a small bowl, stir together mascarpone and honey. Brush one side of each bread slice with butter. Place on work surface, buttered side down, and spread 4 slices with mascarpone mixture. Top equally with Brie. Cover with top halves of bread and press together gently.

2. Place sandwiches on preheated panini grill or in a large skillet over medium heat and cook, turning once if using a skillet, for 3 to 4 minutes or until golden brown and cheese is melted. Serve immediately.

Tiramisù Grilled Cheese

Serves 4

This is a perfect way to get your fix of a classic but complicated Italian specialty without much fuss, but with all of the deliciousness.

Tips

Be sure to serve these sandwiches warm.

If you can't find mascarpone cheese, substitute 4 oz (125 g) cream cheese, 1 tbsp (15 mL) sour cream and 1 tbsp (15 mL) heavy or whipping (35%) cream and blend together until smooth.

- **Panini grill or large skillet**
- **Preheat grill to medium, if using**

2 tbsp	dark rum	30 mL
2 tsp	coffee-flavored liqueur, such as Kahlúa	10 mL
2 tsp	instant coffee granules	10 mL
½ cup	mascarpone cheese (see Tips, left)	125 mL
8	slices Italian bread (½-inch/1 cm thick slices)	8
2 tbsp	butter, softened	30 mL

1. In a small microwave-safe bowl, combine rum, liqueur and coffee granules. Microwave for 20 seconds. Stir until coffee granules dissolve. Let cool for 5 minutes

2. In a medium bowl, combine cooled coffee mixture and mascarpone, stirring to combine.

3. Brush one side of each bread slice with butter. Place on a work surface, buttered side down. Spread 4 bread slices equally with mascarpone mixture. Cover with remaining bread slices, buttered side up, and press together gently.

4. Place sandwiches on preheated panini grill or large skillet over medium heat and cook, turning once if using a skillet, for 3 to 4 minutes or until golden brown and cheese is melted. Serve immediately.

Grilled Chocolate and Goat Cheese

Serves 4

The combination of chocolate and goat cheese is so decadent in this dessert.

- Panini grill or large skillet
- Preheat panini grill to medium, if using

8	slices brioche (½-inch/1 cm thick slices)	8
2 tbsp	butter, softened	30 mL
1 cup	Goat Cheese and Honey Spread (page 194) (see Tip, page 211)	250 mL
1 cup	mini semisweet chocolate chips, melted	250 mL
¼ cup	chopped pecans, optional	60 mL

1. Brush one side of each bread slice equally with butter. Place bread on a work surface, buttered side down. Spread 8 bread slices equally with Goat Cheese Honey Spread. Spread 4 slices with melted chocolate, and pecans, if desired. Cover with remaining bread slices, buttered side up, and press together gently.

2. Place sandwiches on preheated panini grill, or in a large skillet over medium heat and cook, turning once if using a skillet, for 3 to 4 minutes or until golden brown and cheese is melted. Serve immediately.

Grilled Blackberry and Brie

*I can't think of
two more favorite
ingredients than
blackberry preserves
and Brie. And on a
brioche, it doesn't get
much better than that.*

Tip

Use any of your favorite
preserves in this
recipe. Sprinkle with
confectioner's (icing) sugar
before serving for extra
sweetness.

- **Panini grill or large skillet**
- **Preheat panini grill to medium, if using**

8	slices brioche (1/2-inch/1 cm thick slices)	8
2 tbsp	butter, softened	30 mL
1/2 cup	blackberry preserves or jam	125 mL
4 oz	Brie, thinly sliced	125 g

1. Brush one side of each bread slice equally with butter. Place bread on a work surface, buttered side down. Spread 8 bread slices equally with preserves. Top 4 slices with Brie. Cover with remaining bread slices, buttered side up, and press together gently.

2. Place sandwiches on preheated panini grill or in a large skillet over medium heat and cook, turning once if using a skillet, for 3 to 4 minutes or until golden brown and cheese is melted. Serve immediately.

Grilled Mascarpone, Banana and Honey

Mascarpone is an Italian cheese made from cream. It works well in almost any dessert grilled cheese recipe like this simple one with bananas and honey.

Tip

To toast pecans: Spread nuts in a single layer on a baking sheet. Bake in a preheated 350°F (180°C) oven, stirring occasionally, for 10 to 15 minutes.

½ cup	mascarpone cheese	125 mL
¼ cup	liquid honey	60 mL
½ tsp	ground cinnamon	2 mL
4	8-inch (20 cm) flour or whole wheat tortillas	4
3	bananas, thinly sliced	3
½ cup	chopped pecans, toasted (see Tip, left)	125 mL
2 tbsp	butter	30 mL

1. In a small bowl, combine mascarpone, honey and cinnamon.

2. Place tortillas on a work surface. Spread mascarpone mixture equally down center of each tortilla. Top with sliced bananas and nuts. Fold tortilla in half.

3. Heat butter in a large skillet over medium heat. Add wraps and cook for 3 minutes or until lightly browned. Cut into wedges and serve immediately.

Variation

Grilled Mascarpone, Banana and Nut Butter: Add ¼ cup (60 mL) chocolate-hazelnut spread or peanut, almond or cashew butters to these wraps after you add the mascarpone cheese.

Brie and Raspberry Panini with Hazelnut Spread

Serves 4

This is a new twist on the classic combination of chocolate and Brie. The surprising freshness from the raspberries really puts it over the top.

- Panini grill or large skillet
- Preheat panini grill to medium, if using

8	slices sourdough bread (½-inch/1 cm thick slices)	8
2 tbsp	butter, softened	30 mL
¼ cup	chocolate-hazelnut spread, such as Nutella	60 mL
4 oz	Brie, thinly sliced	125 g
¼ cup	fresh raspberries, chopped (2 oz/60 g)	60 mL

1. Brush one side of each bread slice equally with butter. Place bread on a work surface, buttered side down. Spread 4 bread slices equally with chocolate-hazelnut spread. Top with Brie and raspberries. Cover with remaining bread slices, buttered side up, and press together gently.

2. Place sandwiches on preheated panini grill or in a large skillet over medium heat and cook, turning once if using a skillet, for 3 to 4 minutes or until golden brown and cheese is melted. Serve immediately.

Variation

Substitute 8 brioche slices for sourdough bread.

Grilled Balsamic, Strawberry and Mascarpone Sandwich

Serves 4

Mascarpone and strawberry is a sublime combination, delectable enough for dessert, but also perfect for breakfast.

- **Panini grill or large skillet**
- **Preheat panini grill to medium, if using**

2 tsp	granulated sugar	10 mL
1 tsp	ground cinnamon	5 mL
6 tbsp	mascarpone cheese	90 mL
1 tsp	balsamic vinegar	5 mL
8	slices Italian bread (1/2-inch/1 cm thick slices)	8
2 tbsp	butter, softened	30 mL
4 tbsp	strawberry preserves or jam	60 mL

1. In a small bowl, combine sugar and cinnamon. Set aside.

2. In another small bowl, combine mascarpone cheese and balsamic vinegar.

3. Spread one side of each bread slice with butter. Place on a work surface, buttered side down. Spread 4 bread slices equally with mascarpone mixture. Spread remaining 4 slices with preserves. Cover with remaining bread slices, buttered side up, and press together gently.

4. Place sandwiches on preheated panini grill or in a large skillet over medium heat and cook, turning once if using a skillet, for 3 to 4 minutes or until golden brown. Sprinkle with cinnamon sugar mixture. Serve immediately.

Variation

You can use white sandwich bread instead of Italian bread.

Dark Chocolate and Banana Grilled Cheese

Bananas and dark chocolate paired with mascarpone make a fabulous, easy dessert. Cut into mini slices to serve to a kids as well as adults.

Tips

Feel free to use any type of chocolate in this recipe. I like to use bittersweet or dark chocolate for its smoky, rich taste and health benefits.

To melt chopped chocolate: Place chocolate in a microwave-safe bowl. Microwave on Medium (50%) power for 2 to 3 minutes, stirring ever 30 seconds, until chocolate is melted.

- **Panini grill or large skillet**
- **Preheat panini grill to medium, if using**

¼ cup	butter, softened	60 mL
8	slices challah bread (½-inch/1 cm thick) slices	8
½ cup	mascarpone cheese	125 mL
2	bananas, thinly sliced	2
4 oz	bittersweet (dark) chocolate, chopped, melted (see Tips, left)	125 g

1. Brush one side of each bread slice with butter. Place on a work surface, buttered side down, and spread 4 bread slices with mascarpone cheese. Top equally with banana slices and drizzle evenly with chocolate. Top with remaining bread slice, buttered side up, and press together gently.

2. Place sandwiches on preheated panini grill or in a large skillet and cook, turning once if using a skillet, for 3 to 4 minutes or until golden brown and cheese is melted. Serve immediately.

Pear Ricotta Panini

My talented friend Caroline came up with this recipe. It's a great way to showcase pears for a lovely fall dessert or even breakfast.

Tip

To toast almonds: Place almonds in a small dry skillet over medium-high heat, stirring frequently, for about 2 minutes or until golden and toasted.

- **Panini grill or large skillet**
- **Preheat panini grill to medium heat, if using**

2 tsp	granulated sugar	10 mL
1 tsp	ground cinnamon	5 mL
6 tbsp	ricotta cheese	90 mL
1 tbsp	grated orange zest	15 mL
4	slices Italian bread ($\frac{1}{2}$-inch/1 cm thick slices)	4
$\frac{1}{4}$ cup	butter, softened	60 mL
2	medium firm, ripe pears, thinly sliced	2
$\frac{1}{4}$ cup	sliced almonds, toasted (see Tip, left)	60 mL
2 tsp	liquid honey	10 mL

1. In a small bowl, combine sugar and cinnamon. Set aside.

2. In another small bowl, combine ricotta cheese and orange zest.

3. Brush one side of each bread slice with butter. Place on a work surface, buttered side down, and spread ricotta mixture equally over 4 bread slices. Top with sliced pears and almonds. Drizzle with honey. Cover with remaining bread slices, buttered side up, and press together gently.

4. Place sandwiches on preheated panini grill or in a large skillet over medium heat and cook, turning once if using a skillet, for 2 to 3 minutes or until golden brown. Sprinkle with cinnamon sugar. Serve immediately.

Raspberry and Chocolate Grilled Cheese

This five-ingredient recipe is easy as can be, flavored with raspberry and chocolate.

Tip

To quickly melt chocolate: Place chocolate chips in a microwave-safe bowl. Microwave on Medium (50%) power, for 1 minute, stirring every 30 seconds, or until chocolate is melted.

- Panini grill or large skillet
- Preheat Panini grill to medium heat, if using

4	croissants, split	4
2 tbsp	butter, softened	60 mL
½ cup	mascarpone or light cream cheese	125 mL
½ cup	seedless raspberry preserves or jam	125 mL
1 cup	regular or mini semisweet chocolate chips, melted (see Tip, left)	250 mL

1. Brush each side of croissant with butter. Place on a work surface, buttered side down, and spread 4 halves evenly with cream cheese and raspberry preserves. Drizzle with chocolate. Cover with top halves of croissant, buttered side up, and press together gently.

2. Place sandwiches on preheated panini grill or in a large skillet over medium heat and cook, turning once if using a skillet, 3 to 4 minutes or until golden brown. Serve immediately.

Variation

Substitute 8 sourdough bread slices (½-inch/ 1 cm thick) for the croissants in this dish.

Open-Faced Blueberry and Almond Sandwich

I love the combination of blueberry and almonds. This makes a sweet, light dessert on a warm summer afternoon or evening.

Tip

Goat Cheese and Honey Spread is easy to make, but you can buy it in the deli or cheese section of well-stocked supermarkets or cheese shops in tubs. I particularly like the Belle Chèvre brand, made in Alabama.

4	slices sourdough bread (1/2-inch/1 cm thick slices), toasted	4
2 tbsp	butter, softened	30 mL
1/4 cup	Goat Cheese and Honey Spread (page 194) or store-bought (see Tip, left)	60 mL
1 cup	fresh blueberries	250 mL
1/4 cup	chopped toasted almonds (see Tip, page 209)	60 mL
1/4 cup	sifted confectioner's (icing) sugar, optional	60 mL

1. Brush one side of each bread slice with butter. Place on a work surface, buttered side down. Spread bread slices equally with goat cheese spread. Top with blueberries and almonds. Place bread slices in a large skillet over medium heat and cook for 3 minutes or until bottoms are lightly browned. Sprinkle with confectioner's sugar, if desired. Serve immediately.

Variation

Use brioche instead of sourdough bread for a richer dessert.

Dessert Crêpes

My best friend, Lisa, from Nashville, makes these for company all of the time, and she always receives rave reviews. I was so excited for her to share this recipe in my book.

Tips

You can make the crêpe batter ahead of time and refrigerate for up to 8 hours.

Don't flip crêpes too early. Wait until the edges begin to brown.

1 cup	all-purpose flour	250 mL
2	eggs	2
1/2 cup	milk	125 mL
2 tbsp	butter, melted	30 mL
1/2 tsp	vanilla extract	2 mL
1/4 tsp	salt	1 mL
2 tbsp	vegetable oil, divided	30 mL

Cream Cheese Snow Filling

1	package (8 oz/250 g) cream cheese, softened	1
2 cups	confectioner's (icing) sugar	500 mL
2 tbsp	grated lemon zest	30 mL
1 cup	heavy or whipping (35%) cream	250 mL
	Sliced strawberries or blueberries	

1. In a large bowl, whisk together flour and eggs. Gradually add milk and 1/2 cup (125 mL) water, stirring to combine. Beat in butter, vanilla and salt until smooth.

2. In large skillet, heat 1 tbsp (15 mL) of the oil over medium heat. Pour 1/4 cup (60 mL) of the batter into skillet for each crêpe. Tilt pan in a circular motion so batter covers surface of pan. Cook crêpes for 2 minutes or until bottom is golden brown. Loosen with a spatula. Flip and cook other side for 2 minutes or until golden brown.

3. *Cream Cheese Snow Filling:* Meanwhile, in a medium bowl, using an electric mixer, beat cream cheese until soft. Blend in sugar and beat until creamy. Add lemon zest.

4. Fill each crêpe evenly with Cream Cheese Snow Filling. Fold in half. Add remaining 1 tbsp (15 mL) of oil to skillet over medium heat. Heat both sides of crêpe for 2 minutes or until filling is warmed.

5. In a separate bowl, whip cream until slightly thickened. Serve over warm crêpes with berries.

Library and Archives Canada Cataloguing in Publication

Lewis, Alison, 1967–
    150 best grilled cheese sandwiches / Alison Lewis.

Includes index.
ISBN 978-0-7788-0412-3

1. Cooking (Cheese). 2. Sandwiches. 3. Cookbooks.
I. Title. II. Title: One hundred fifty best grilled cheese sandwiches.

TX759.5.C48L48 2012   641.6'73   C2012-902801-0

Index

(v) = variation

C